BEING TOGETHER

BEING TOGETHER

PRACTICAL WISDOM FOR LOVING
YOURSELF AND YOUR PARTNER

BY PADMA GORDON M.Ed

NEW DEGREE PRESS

BEING TOGETHER

Practical Wisdom for Loving Yourself and Your Partner

Image for front cover: Konrad Knell

ISBN

978-1-64137-969-4   *Paperback*

978-1-64137-847-5   *Kindle Ebook*

978-1-64137-848-2   *Digital Ebook*

To my partner, Gautam, for sharing the sweetness of his gentle heart, for staying the course, and being willing to grow and discover the true nature of love with me. And to my beloved daughter, Meera, for being patient with her Mom as she wrote this book. May this labor of love serve as a roadmap to guide you and your generation gracefully along as you discover the divine ecstasy of being in a deeply loving relationship.

CONTENTS

———

"For small creatures such as we, the universe is only bearable through love."

ACKNOWLEDGEMENTS

Firstly, I am deeply grateful to everyone who has contributed their wisdom and personal stories to this book. Thank you for being open-hearted and vulnerable with me, for sharing intimate stories—stories that don't always make you look good, but rather showcase your growing edges. This unites us in our humanity and lets us know we are not alone.

This book is about evolutionary growth. It's about self-discovery through being in and staying in a healthy, non-damaging relationship all while upholding individual, inner integrity. Thank you for taking the time to love yourself; who we are in a relationship *is* who we are with ourselves.

For your insight and wisdom, thank you to: Jeanne and Bill Rachles, Danny and Nancy Katz, Gabriela and Solomon Masala, Tom and Andrea Pinkson, Kathy Altman and Lori Salzman, Tom Herington and Gary Topper, Shakti Shen and Moksha MutiMan, Marc Grossman and Noelle Adamo, and Clark Tate. Jen and Jay, as well as Michael and Josie, are real couples who asked me to use pseudonyms for them. Deep thanks also to my dear friend, Dr. Christa Santangelo, for her unbridled support and wisdom.

One of the most poignant and humbling discoveries I made while writing my first book is that although I appear to be its author, this book was really written by many voices. I am grateful for each of you who faithfully attended my Zoom group to offer input: Roz and David Gordon, MaryAnne and Jeff Pollack, David Goodman and Raychil Phillips. And, to the many others who read chapters, helped me find just the right word, and were present with me through this potent and arduous process—including our dog, Buddy. He lovingly snuggled against me, his warm body acting as support, propping up my computer as I spent many a late-night writing on the couch.

And last but certainly not least, I want to express gratitude to: my parents, extended family, close friends, community of amazing book supporters who believed in me enough to purchase advance copies, and my ex-partners for schooling me. Also to Professor Koester for his Book Creator's vision, my publisher and dedicated staff at New Degree Press, my wonderful editors, Karina and Heather, and my brilliant niece, Eden Arielle, for being my editing ally and offering her wise soul's insights. Finally, to the supremely generous, talented, and deeply thoughtful Katrin Snow, who swooped in at the last moment to offer her exquisite editorial eyes and heart which helped shape this book into what it is. I am humbled in the face of love's magnificent generosity. Now, let us begin.

INTRODUCTION

Long-term relationships are epic challenges. They ask us to be real and to reveal our magnificence as well as our shadows to another person, all of which render us vulnerable. They invite us to be present and discerning. Ultimately, they can serve to evolve us into the best, most loving version of ourselves.

Over time, a committed relationship can become a spiritual practice, the kind that helps in learning self-love and awakening to your true nature. If you are committed to the cause, a long-term relationship can be a container within which you can evolve into the person you were meant to be.

As we travel through the landscape of this book, I will share valuable lessons from people who have had thriving long-term relationships, the principles which have made them work, and some simple steps you can take to implement them yourself.

YOU CAN HAVE A HEALTHY RELATIONSHIP

So many of us want a healthy relationship, but we may not have had good role models. I personally did not, although I always knew my parents loved each other and their relationship has endured for more than six decades. However, the volatility of their dynamic is not something I want to emulate.

My question became: *If you haven't had positive role models, can you have a successful long-term relationship?* After speaking to many long-term couples and taking a deep dive into some of the cutting-edge research on modern love and relationships, I believe the answer is: *yes, if you are willing to go the distance.*

I have spent the past few years studying lifetime love relationships, both in my private counseling practice as well as personally, especially since I have been in a fairly new and deeply committed relationship with a wonderful man. I have worked with many couples and witnessed that radical shifts are possible when people are willing to be vulnerable and listen attentively to one another.

The statistics are admittedly daunting: *"42–45 percent of first marriages end in divorce; 60 percent of second marriages end in divorce; 73 percent of third marriages end in divorce."* Furthermore, *"the United States has the third highest divorce rate in the world, with 4.34 divorces per 1,000 people,"* according to McKinley Irvin Family Law.[1]

Still, there is hope for all you hopeless romantics. My invitation to you is to open up to unknown possibilities and trust you are exactly where you need to be. Lifetime love is possible, as long as you are up for the challenge.

---

1 "32 Shocking Divorce Statistics," *Family Law Blog*, McKinley Irvin Family Law, updated 2018.

That said, your "relationship success" may look very different from what you thought a relationship "should" look like. Many of us believe, *"When I find my soulmate, I will be happy."* We imagine someone else will make us happy—a fundamental misunderstanding. The notion that a prince (or princess or variation thereupon) on a white horse will whisk you away to a far-off land where you'll live happily ever after in a magnificent castle where spring is always in full bloom is a Disney-induced trance.

Realizing you are in a trance is a wakeup call; it may feel like having a bucket of ice water poured right over your head. I've had several long-term relationships over the past forty years and now recognize that projecting perfection or wanting a relationship to be one long honeymoon doesn't work. Honestly, it's a relief. In my current relationship, I am staying put, instead of following my old program, which was to cut and run when things got tough—because I am committed.

It's not as simple as finding *"the one."* What if, rather than clinging to the idea of meeting your ideal mate, you turn your attention inward?

I propose you find someone with whom you have enough in common, good chemistry, and overlapping values; choose someone who is willing to grow, someone with whom you can evolve. In a healthy relationship, both partners are committed to growing as individuals *and* as a couple. Psychologists like Gay Hendricks and his wife, Kathlyn Hendricks, talk about a *"relationship as a path to enlightenment and enlivenment."*

If you would like to experience a long-term committed relationship, this book for you. If you are ready to be present, discover your true nature, and embark on the journey to an intimate partnership, please continue reading. Whether you are in your twenties or thirties looking for guidance on how to embark on this magnificent voyage, in your forties or fifties and have all but given up hope, or in your sixties or seventies and want to develop your capacity for loving, then then this book is for you.

The United States has finally achieved marriage equality and has become more accepting of households where both partners have the same gender. In a time of increasing gender inclusion, this book intends to address human relations, rather than partnerships based on normative gender identity or sexual orientation. That said, most of the people I have interviewed for this book identify as heterosexual, which I realize is only one perspective. However, the principles I discuss here were common to all of the couples I interviewed, regardless of orientation. My hope is that the practical wisdom I share will serve each of us, as human beings wanting connection and love.

I have interviewed numerous couples who—through working on themselves and staying centered in their coupledom—have maintained successful, loving relationships. Theirs are the valuable insights I will be sharing with you. These people have been willing to sweat it out, while keeping their hearts open. Let's learn from their successes and failures by taking a closer look at how they have thrived and make the practice of loving our own.

CHAPTER 1

A FOUNDATION FOR THE JOURNEY

———

"All journeys have secret destinations of which the traveler is unaware."

— MARTIN BUBER

This book is intended to take you on a journey into the heart of what's necessary to have and maintain a *thriving relationship*. To begin, I will invite you to engage with some psychological theories and ideas related to mindfulness and mysticism. Since this realm is infinitely vast, I invite you to enter with a beginner's mind. Pry the hinges off the trap doors of your mind and receive the winds of wisdom and wonder. Please don't try too hard to grab hold of or remember things. Trust that whatever is important for you will sink in. In my experience, grasping hinders true understanding. Relax and *allow* the information to come in. Breathe. This book is intended to nourish your heart and soul. Sit back and savor.

WHERE I'M COMING FROM

My intention is to share insight into the human condition that I have gathered firsthand over the past forty years—throughout my own contemplative journey and my experience as a teacher and spiritual counselor.

I am an eternal student of life. I have studied relationships from psychological, sociological, and spiritual perspectives. On the spiritual side I have cultivated wisdom and compassion through maintaining a consistent meditation practice, which, combined with studies of esoteric traditions, allows me to be of true service.

Building on this, I will break down some fundamental psychological concepts as they pertain to relationships and offer insights and reflections based on my studies of acclaimed research of psychologists such as John Gottman, Stan Tatkin, and Sue Johnson. Together, these psychologists have collectively done clinical studies on relationships equating to nearly a hundred years. I am grateful to them for having dug in so deeply and for amassing a vast amount of research that has been so useful in my own life and relationships.

Last but not least, I have been in a series of relationships for over thirty years. However, I come to you not as someone who has been happily married for a quarter century, but rather as a human invested in discovering what it takes to have a healthy, long-term relationship. It's true, we teach—or in my case, write—about what we need to learn.

During this writing process, my relationship has morphed into a truly great relationship. I attribute this to having implemented the ideas and practices written about here.

I envision that, with the help of this book and the practices in it, your own relationship will flourish and become a loving, safe, and nourishing container in which to heal and evolve. And, if you already have a thriving relationship, may it flower to the next level and may you be surprised at the depths of love that continue to reveal themselves. Most important, regardless of where you are on your relationship journey, enjoy!

MAPPING IT OUT

I will begin by exploring the developmental psychology concept of attachment—after all, it forms the basis for how we show up in a relationship. Beyond what's offered here, there are many great books solely dedicated to attachment theory which are listed in the resources section at the end of the book. If the attachment work resonates for you, please explore it more deeply. With that, let us dive in.

WHAT IS ATTACHMENT?

When we enter into an intimate relationship as an adult, our early childhood or *"attachment"* styles—and the ways we have organized our emotional responses and assumptions—show up. It's similar to when the roots of a tree grow up and around a big rock. The rock is the wound. Our wounds are the places where we did not get what we needed from our parents or primary attachment figure. Enter *"attachment theory."*

According to developmental psychology theorists, "attachment theory states that a strong emotional and physical attachment to at least one primary caregiver is critical to personal development."[2] John Bowlby and Mary Ainsworth, twentieth century developmental psychologists and psychiatrists, first coined the term after studying developmental mindsets in children from various backgrounds.

A strong attachment happens when, as an infant, you receive love and touch from primary caregivers. This creates an internal sense of safety and security, provides a stable foundation on which to move through life, and informs how you act later on in romantic partnerships.

Without this kind of formative relationship in place, Bowlby discovered that *"a great deal of developmental energy was expended in the search for stability and security."*[3]

What matters is how much you were held and tended to. In other words, the quality of attention you were given. For instance, if your mother was often distracted or overwhelmed, she may not have been able to hold you for as long as you needed in order to be soothed. This could easily be the case if you came from a large family. What mother could possibly be fully present with each of her seven children? In this case, you might later enter into a relationship expecting to get very little from your partner. Since this is all you have ever known, it makes a lot of sense that you would choose a partner whose capacity for giving is limited. We bring our early childhood imprints into our intimate adult relationships.

---

2   "Attachment Theory," *Developmental Psychology,* Psychologist World, accessed February 5, 2020.

3   Ibid.

If this is all new to you, you may want to take some time to reflect on how your attachment style has given rise to certain ways of being in relationships. This would be a good moment to notice how your behaviors are being informed by early childhood imprints. When you become aware of your unconscious patterning, it is as if it has been brought into the light. When things are illuminated, you are free to make conscious choices about how you want to relate as an adult in a relationship. Awareness is powerful and, in my experience, it is the key to freedom.

BONDING AND HOW YOU CAME TO BE YOU

Your attachment style, formed during the first eighteen or so months of your life, largely dictates your later ability to participate in a loving relationship. This is because, according to couples therapist and attachment expert Stan Tatkin, Psy.D., "your early experiences with attachment create an instructional blueprint that remains stored in your body; that blueprint determines your basic relational wiring along with your sense of safety."[4]

The quality of the bonding experience you had with your primary attachment figure determines your particular *"attachment style."* Being held by a responsive and present attachment figure calms the nervous system. Imagine how a baby relaxes when they feel safe and held.

In other words, the atmosphere in which you grew up determines your ideas about what it means to love and be loved.

---

4   "Wired for Love Quotes," Goodreads, accessed February 6, 2020.

We are shaped by our early life experiences. As infants, we are a bit like lumps of soft clay. Tatkin confirms this: "What happens is that as adults, we transfer our primary attachments from our parents on to our partners."[5]

This is where most of us begin to feel challenged in a relationship. We are, in a sense, all projecting our history onto our adult partners. A relationship is a place to learn about love and the way we were loved impacts our ability to show up when we are in one. As Tatkin also says:

> "We learn to love ourselves precisely because we have experienced being loved by someone. We learn to take care of ourselves because somebody has taken care of us. Our self-worth and self-esteem also develop because of other people."[6]

Ultimately, your partner is a catalyst for you to see and know yourself more fully. The true work happens on the inside. It's not about what *they* do or don't do. It's about how *you* respond. Your partner will give you plenty of opportunities to learn how to respond skillfully, which means that they become a catalyst for your healing and you become one for theirs. A relationship is a mutually beneficial agreement to evolve.

An attachment style is sometimes called an emotional relating style. If you want to have a thriving relationship, it is

---

5   C.J. Liu, "How to Build Intimacy? (Stan Tatkin)," *Fire It Up With CJ*, June 22, 2015.

6   Goodreads, "Wired for Love Quotes."

important to understand your partner's emotional relating style (as well as your own). Investing in understanding these dynamics from the beginning will save you loads of time later on. Understanding gives rise to the ability to empathize, which in turn makes it easier to build rapport. When you know how to relate to your partner in a way that works for them and vice versa, it becomes easier to build a stable connection.

So, be patient and study your partner. Remember that they are different from you, and that what makes you happy is not necessarily what will make them smile. I will discuss various "love languages" later on in the book in more detail.

GETTING TO KNOW YOUR STYLE

There are three primary attachment styles. Stan Tatkin has a model for describing these which I find is easily accessible, so I will be using it in addition to the classical terms used in developmental psychology.

I have summarized Tatkin's model and added my own examples below. Once you hear about these three different styles, you might feel like you'd prefer to be one over another. The fact is, though, they all have their pros and cons. What's most important is to acknowledge which attachment style you have, so that you can understand yourself more fully and learn to work with your strengths and weaknesses. Remember, your attachment style is based on formative family culture.

The three primary attachment styles are:

- Secure

- Anxious

- Avoidant

In Tatkin's model, each of these attachment styles corresponds to Anchors, Waves, and Islands, respectively. Please note that the fourth attachment style, Disorganized, is particular to people who have experienced early childhood trauma, including various types of abuse. This attachment style falls beyond the scope of this book, though I include some suggestions for delving deeper in the resource section at the end of the book.

ANCHORS—SECURE

Let us begin with the Anchors, or those who have a secure attachment style. If you are an Anchor, you are most likely a happy person who is adaptable and willing to commit in a relationship. How did you come to be this way? The Anchor culture that you were raised in valued relationships highly and prioritized positive human interactions. This means that people considered each other before taking an action. They asked themselves, *"Will this work for everyone?"*

Your parents were likely communicative, attuned (they listened and responded with love), and noticed when you were upset. When you cried, they picked you up and lovingly held you until you were calm. Your infant nervous system was able to co-regulate with their nervous system, which helped you to relax and feel safe.

At least one of your parents or primary caregivers was present and responded with consistency. They treated each other and others in your family with respect and kindness—at least most of the time. Basically, you grew up in a healthy environment where you felt safe, cared for, and loved. This is wonderful and, as a result of your experience, you are now able to offer kindness and presence to your partner. You respond in a timely way when they text you, you are easy to be with, and people generally like you.

Anchors are not perfect people, though. They can be triggered into knee-jerk reactions just like anyone else. Although it is a gift to walk through the world feeling at ease in your own skin, it's best not to idealize the securely attached. They may seem to have an easier time navigating the world than others, but that's not always the case.

It is important to mention that when you are in a healthy relationship with a person who has a secure attachment style, you can "*earn a secure attachment*" through healthy relationship dynamics. Take comfort in the fact that you can heal your childhood hurts in a stable present-day partnership.

WAVES—ANXIOUS

If you are a Wave, or someone who is insecurely anxious, you probably had a primary caregiver who was also anxious or often preoccupied. Maybe one parent was fearful of the other or perhaps someone in your household exhibited erratic behavior, creating a feeling of instability and hypervigilance. Being held by someone who was distracted may have caused you to feel unsettled, rather than soothed. In fact, you may have developed a child's misunderstanding that it was *your* job to emotionally take care of the caregiver, instead of the other way around. Your relationship with your primary caregiver was, in short, upside-down.

As an infant, you felt responsible. Infants are pre-verbal so this was not a thought—rather it was an intuitive or a felt-sense that your caregiver needed something from you. You were held by at least one person in your home and there was some focus on interaction, but it was perhaps inconsistent. You may be someone who remembers a parent watching you do a cartwheel that you had been practicing in gymnastics class. However, you may have felt disappointed and insignificant when you noticed that they were watching you and simultaneously doing other things.

When you are in a relationship, you tend to experience doubts about your partner along with fears of being abandoned, and you can be clingy at times. You have a need to talk about your feelings a lot. You process your feelings externally and you may even find yourself saying something to trigger your partner just to get their attention. The truth is, you are wanting to feel loved.

In a relationship, you may be prone to making threats. Sometimes when you get angry, a self-protective mechanism kicks in and you push your partner away. You may be afraid to be all in because your partner might leave you. Be gentle with yourself if this is resonating as your attachment style. Your first step is to recognize how the pattern works. Be compassionate with yourself if you cannot relax and trust the love that your partner offers. You are responding to them based on the fact that your primary caregiver's love was ambiguous. They were there and simultaneously not there for you.

On the flip side, you are giving and generous. You love to take care of people, which makes sense because you learned how to do it very early on in life. This may mean that your primary caregiver leaned on you as a confidante when you were a child. You learned that your job was to take care of them and hold space, even though in a healthy parent-child relationship it would be the other way around.

ISLANDS—AVOIDANT

Last but not least, we have the Islands, or the insecurely avoidant attachment style. If you are an Island, you probably spent a lot of time alone as a child and as a result are fiercely independent and self-reliant. You know how to take care of yourself and are one of those folks who "doesn't need other people." You could happily live alone in a cabin on a mountainside. In a relationship, you need a lot of space. If you're living with a partner, you might want to have your own bedroom so you have the option to retreat when you feel the need.

You generally don't need a lot of physical touch and probably grew up in a family lacking in that kind of affection. Sometimes in a relationship, you might feel smothered by your partner's touch rather than nourished by it. You might also feel like your partner is pulling on you when they want to see you several nights a week. For you, less is more. I have known Islands who were content to see their partner once or twice a week at most. For instance, it would work well for you as an Island to live in Colorado while your partner lives in Vermont. It might be plenty of contact to see your partner for long weekends or romantic rendezvous, and the day-to-day sharing of life and a home with your partner can easily feel overwhelming to you.

As an Island, you may tend to be quite logical and rational, and if your partner asks you, "How are you feeling?" you may not know. When asked about their feelings, Islands have been known to say, " I'll need to get back to you on that." It's easy for an Island to feel trapped in a relationship. Conversely, when they are given space, they might be more inclined to lean in rather than retreat.

Relating with anyone takes skill, and relating to Islands and Waves ups the ante. These groups are more delicate and less resilient than Anchors and need to be treated with extra care. They didn't get what the Anchors got from their families, so they feel less safe and tend to be more reactive. Again, everyone is lovable. Getting to know how your partner works will make the practice of loving them easier, and there will be fewer bumps in the road.

A TWO-PERSON SECURE SYSTEM

It is important to define the "two-person secure system" since I will be referring to it a lot throughout this book and since it's essential to having a thriving relationship. Couples therapist Stan Tatkin writes:

"Secure functioning refers to an interpersonal system based on principles of true mutuality, collaboration, justice, fairness, and sensitivity. Secure-functioning partners are fully interdependent in the sense that each happily accepts that they are in each other's care."[7]

Particularly for those of us who are Waves and Islands, the safe container of an intimate relationship is a place where we can receive what we most need which is to be seen, heard, and loved by someone who is present. Our partner can effectively serve as a surrogate to assist us in being re-parented. It's not that your partner *is* your parent. It's that when you are in a secure system, they can offer a steady presence of love, a wall to lean on when you are triggered, acting out, or feeling wobbly. The idea is: we make a conscious choice to take care of one another, to protect each other, and to "have each other's backs."

Another important piece that complicates things is that depending upon the person with whom you are in partnership, your attachment style can change. For example, you may have grown up with an Island-like attachment style and then find yourself in partnership with someone who exhibits stronger Island traits than you do. In this situation, you might become relatively more of a Wave and become the one wanting to spend more time together to create a sense of relationship balance. Different dynamics arise with

---

7   Stan Tatkin and Tracey Boldemann-Tatkin, "What Does It Mean to Be in a Secure-Functioning Relationship? and Why Should It Matter to Me?" *Shambhala Mountain Center* (blog), August 14, 2019.

different partners. The interplay between human beings in a relationship is incredibly complicated.

Be patient and kind with yourself as you navigate the tender terrain of loving.

A LITTLE BIT ABOUT THE NEUROBIOLOGY OF LOVE

I would be remiss not to make mention of love's own neurobiology.

Personally, I find it fascinating. Maybe you've heard the vintage song by Frankie Lymon & The Teenagers in which Frankie croons, "*Why do fools fall in love?*" What happens on a neurological level in the brain strongly influences why fools fall in love. When falling in love, our brains essentially get drunk on a "*love cocktail.*" This cocktail takes us over. It triggers a host of "neurochemicals in our brains that are associated with sex-drive, attachment, and partner preference."[8]

Dr. Helen Fisher, who has spent years delving into the neurobiology of love, says, "Love is a complex neurobiological phenomenon, relying on trust, belief, pleasure and reward activities within the brain, i.e., limbic processes. These processes critically involve oxytocin, vasopressin, dopamine, and serotonergic signaling."[9]

---

8 Jacob Devaney, "The Neurobiology of Love and Relationships," *UPLIFT*, January 14, 2016.

9 Tobias Esch and George B. Stefano, "The Neurobiology of Love," *Neuroendocrinology Letters* 26, no. 3 (June 2005): 175.

In Stan Tatkin's book *Your Brain on Love: The Neurobiology of Healthy Relationships*, he explains that, when you fall in love, your brain gets flooded with dopamine, which makes you feel high.[10] You feel exalted and like you're on top of the world. Then, increases in the brain chemical, oxytocin, and the hormone vasopressin come in to make you feel bonded to your partner. It's also helpful that levels of another brain chemical, serotonin, drop.[11] It's as if you are addicted to your partner. You can't stop thinking about them and are waiting to hear from them. Maybe you check your phone every two minutes to see if they've texted or called. Or you wonder what they might be doing and if you should call them or wait for them to call you. If this sounds familiar, it's because you're human and are subject to the *love cocktail* just like the rest of us. These drives hurl us toward procreation. Of course, love, sex, and relationships are not just for procreating; they are also essential for our physical health, personal growth, and spiritual evolution. According to Dr. Helen Fisher:

> "Dopamine is released when we do things that feel good to us. In this case, these things include spending time with loved ones and having sex. High levels of dopamine and a related hormone, norepinephrine, *are released during attraction. These chemicals make us giddy, energetic, and euphoric...*"[12]

---

10   Stan Tatkin, *Your Brain on Love: The Neurobiology of Healthy Relationships*, read by the author, (Louisville: Sounds True Publishing, 2013). Audio CD, 5 hr., 50 min.

11   Giovanna Castro, "The Neuroscience of Love," *Emotion, Brain, & Behavior Laboratory* (blog), December 8, 2014.

12   Katherine Wu, "Love, Actually: The Science Behind Lust, Attraction, and Companionship," *Science in the News*, Harvard University, February 14, 2017.

One might say that being in love is an elevated state, and these feelings of euphoria are deeply related to the love cocktail we have all sipped at one time or another—because it feels so good!

REFLECTION

We just dove into the deep end big time. Let's go over the most essential concepts and definitions we've just covered.

We looked at infant attachment and how it informs the way you behave in an intimate relationship as an adult, then defined the three primary attachment styles: secure, anxious, and avoidant.

Stan Tatkin's model uses oceanic metaphors to describe these, calling them Anchor, Wave, and Island. In a nutshell, Anchors were held and loved plenty while Waves and Islands missed out on this. *Waves* had a distracted primary attachment figure which made them feel anxious, and Islands were raised in a family where the focus was on performance rather than on fostering relationships.

We looked at the two-person secure system and how it forms the foundation for a sustainable, long-term relationship. In this kind of relationship, you have each other's backs. Lastly, we discussed how *love cocktail* neurochemicals in our brains intoxicate us, causing us to fall madly in love.

REMEMBER:

- Understanding both your attachment style and your partner's attachment style will help you have a great relationship.

- Commit to a two-person secure system where you both have each other's backs. It will feel great!

- Recognize that when you fall in love, you have a cocktail of love hormones flooding your brain that may well make you feel like a "fool in love."

A FOUNDATION FOR THE JOURNEY:
REFLECTION AND INTEGRATION WORKSHEET
(IT'S YOUR BOOK, FEEL FREE TO WRITE IN IT.)

I invite you to take a few minutes to write down two things that resonated for you in this chapter. Now, choose one to practice weekly. For the best results, look often at what you've written; your subconscious mind learns through repetition.

_____

_____

_____

_____

_____

_____

_____

_____

_____

_____

CHAPTER 2

THE *We*

___

"Life's not about me; it's about we."

– TONY ROBBINS

Falling in love is a quintessential life experience. It opens us up to being in a relationship. However, the first step to being in a fulfilling relationship is to align with your *own* wholeness so that you enter into this loving dance with a full cup. Being a *We*, or a stable couple, means you consider the other person when you act because you know that your actions have an impact. You recognize that you are no longer flying solo, and you gratefully respond with love and devotion. You cultivate a loving relationship because it feels good, it makes you stronger and more joyful, and because it's good for your physical, mental, and emotional health.

As you will see from the experience of a couple I interviewed— Shakti and Moksha—there are many benefits to being a *We*. "People in happy relationships are less stressed, have better self-esteem, get better sleep, and even live longer than those who are single," Tatkin says.[13]

Shakti and Moksha are the embodiment of a *We*. Their journey together has been amazing since Shakti (who had up to then only been with women partners) met Moksha at fifty-eight. She spent thirty years teaching *tantra*, which integrates loving attention, communication, and spiritual practices into expressions of love. She is now retired and spends her days meditating, diving into love with Moksha, and hiking the hills of Marin County, CA. Shakti's heart beams with love and long ringlet curls frame her face. Her beloved Moksha turned sixty this year and is a tall man with broad shoulders and a well-groomed mustache. They are immensely happy together and are the kind of couple that inspires even the most reluctant of us to want to be in a relationship. They have only been together for a couple of years yet are still deep in the honeymoon phase. How do they do it? They are very protective of their space, prioritize one another, and adore each other madly.

Shakti recently told me that Moksha had moved two van-loads of her things to a vacation home they were visiting for only two nights. *Why?* Because he wanted her to be comfortable. He did this after a full day of physical work because he loves her, her happiness is a priority for him, and because they are in it together. Shakti reciprocates by backing him up with her loving attention; she is his biggest cheerleader, and their mutual devotion is an infinity loop of love.

---

13   Tatkin, *Your Brain on Love*.

Psychologists say that in our couple-based culture, a stable partnership can be an inspiration. Most of us feel good around couples, especially happy couples. They give us a sense of well-being because they summon up a sense of security.

This takes us back to being a child, to the experience of feeling safe and secure when our parents were happy. A happy couple anchors us back to positive memories if our parents were happy together, and if not it offers a window into the reality that loving and happy couples *do* exist.

It's worth noting that you can have a deeply fulfilling life as a single person. I have spent long stretches being single, and these were some of the richest times in my life. You will grow in different, necessary ways when you are single than when you are in a couple.

Jeanne and Bill's relationship is another beautiful example of one in which they each prioritized the other. My Great Aunt Jeanne is ninety-five and in near-perfect health. She is long and lean. Her silvery white hair is always neatly coiffed, her honey green eyes sparkle, and her mind is sharp as a tack. You'd never guess that she is almost a centenarian. Jeanne is one of the most warm-hearted and funny people I've ever known. When I talked to her about her relationship with Bill, she regaled me with tales of the love they shared. In her endearingly thick New York accent, she told me the story of how she and Bill first met at Banner Lodge, an adult summer camp in New York State, and how later they lived in Crown Heights, Brooklyn and Detroit before eventually settling in West Palm Beach, Florida. They were together for sixty-six years. Since Bill's passing five years ago, she lives on her own and maintains regular volunteer work, close friendships, and attends theatre improv classes.

Jeanne and Bill were quite the pair. They traveled through life together in an unquestionable union as a *We*. Jeanne bore four children and has outlived two of them. She is someone who has triumphed against the odds and has the positive attitude of a person who has loved deeply. The nearly seven-decade partnership she had with Bill is extraordinary, and although according to Jeanne it was "far from perfect," through it all their love endured.

She spoke in a quiet and wistful tone, and I felt the tender echoes of their love coursing through her voice. Jeanne said:

> *"We survived, and just being together was*
> *sufficient in knowing that we were going to get*
> *through everything together—which we always*
> *did. There was a lot of kindness on Bill's side. I*
> *always felt that he was looking after me in every*
> *possible way. He was so full of goodness. Bill was*
> *an exceptional human and I felt so fortunate*
> *that he chose to be with me."*

THE COUPLE BUBBLE

Jeanne's notion of "getting through it together" is a powerful one. It expresses a simple idea: together, we will thrive. You will thrive if you *both* tend to your couple bubble. It will hold you in its strength. But remember, a bubble can also be delicate and could burst if left unattended.

Stan Tatkin defines the couple bubble as:

> *"[A]n agreement to put the relationship before*
> *anything and everything else. It means putting*
> *your partner's well-being, self-esteem, and distress*
> *relief first. And it means your partner does the*
> *same for you. You both agree to do it for each other.*
> *Therefore, you say to each other, 'We come first.' In*
> *this way, you cement your relationship. It is like*
> *making a pact or taking a vow, or like reinforcing a*
> *vow you already took with one another."*[14]

I would like to offer an example from my own life that might resonate. I thrive on my partner's full attention, so he has agreed that he will do his best to give me some of his undivided attention each day. This means that when we are on a hike together, he kindly takes his AirPods out to have a conversation because listening to music while talking to me is simply not the same as being fully present. Our agreement is to prioritize each other's well-being.

A *We* actually enhances our ability to evolve. In order to grow, you need to feel securely held. You need to know your partner has your back. You may also find you are capable of accomplishing more and being more fully yourself when you are in a couple. The saying "the whole is greater than the sum of its parts" applies when you are together as a *We*.

Tatkin puts it this way: "Your personal growth depends on your relationship remaining safe and secure at all times,

---

14 Goodreads, "Wired for Love Quotes."

because if either of you feel the least bit unsafe, untrusting, or insecure, you won't have the internal resources for personal growth. Instead, your mind and body will be preoccupied by doubt and threat."[15]

HERE IS A SIMPLE PRACTICE TO SUPPORT YOU IN BEING ROOTED AND FEELING CENTERED IN YOURSELF: Set a timer for three minutes. Take a wide stance and bend your knees slightly. Make sure that your knees are bent enough so you are using your muscles, but not so much that it hurts your joints. Listen to your body. Place all ten fingertips lightly together so that your hands and arms form a circle. Your hands should be roughly at the height of your heart. Breathe in and out through your nose. Drop your weight and keep your heart open. This practice will strengthen your ability to *be in yourself*; a side benefit is that your physical body will be stronger, too.

Staying rooted in yourself—through meditation or other forms of self-care—and spending quality time with your partner are both ways to build a foundation of trust. These methods allow you to keep your heart open and embrace challenges when they arise. Creating safety in a relationship is a gradual process, one in which you must invest your time and devotion. When you do, your relationship will become a bountiful garden to feed and sustain you.

Living as a *We* has many elements. To recap: be in integrity with yourself as you engage with your partner, prioritize

---

15   "We Do Quotes," Goodreads, accessed January 18, 2020.

your relationship, take care of your partner, and consistently love and protect them. When you both do this, you create a secure environment in which to grow.

Next, I would like to introduce you to the idea of doing the "small things."

DO THE SMALL THINGS FOR BIG RESULTS

Dr. John Gottman, PhD, has studied relationships for nearly four decades and emphasizes the importance of making deposits in your emotional bank account as a couple. He has described this action as *doing small things often*. "*Successful long-term relationships are created through small words, small gestures, and small acts,*" he says.[16]

Throughout their relationship, Jeanne and Bill did many small things for each other. Jeanne told me that if they went into a store and she admired something, saying, "That's cute. What a nice ring," Bill would pull out a wad of cash and—with his inimitable grin and a twist of his gray mustache—he would buy it for her on the spot. He was a generous soul and his adoration for Jeanne ran deep. She felt the same way about him, and still does. They built their relationship through small actions and intentional gestures. When you have your antennas up for what your partner needs and what brings them joy, you reinforce the foundation of your relationship.

"The idea is that small, intentional, consistent efforts over time will profoundly transform the trajectory of your relationship,"

---

16   " Eight Dates Quotes," Goodreads, accessed January 18, 2020.

says psychologist and relationship expert John Gottman. "And just like actual banking, it makes the most sense to start early. Small is easy."[17]

It's important to take these small actions daily. Maybe it means you thank your partner for taking out the trash or making dinner. Offer them an appreciative smile or a brief handwritten note. Maybe you set a reminder on your calendar to call your partner from work to let them know you are thinking about them. Send them a text with some heart emojis or an email telling them how awesome you think they are. These are some simple things that you can do, and believe me: your relationship will benefit.

I know that since my partner has started calling me from work in the afternoons to leave short, loving messages, things have been sweeter between us. I appreciate the effort he is making to connect. It doesn't even really matter if we actually talk; it's the fact that he is sending some of his positive, loving energy my way and letting me know that he's thinking about me. When he does this, it enlivens our connection and when I feel this, I relax.

There is science behind this. Stan Tatkin talks about the process of being "tethered to one another," a feeling that is a hallmark of solid relationships.[18] This does not mean that you are attached at the hip. "[Being tethered] means that you are feeling secure and settled in your relationship,"

17   Zach Brittle, "The Positive Perspective," *The Gottman Institute* (blog), April 8, 2015.

18   Goodreads, "Wired for Love Quotes."

he writes. When this happens, "our brain's raphe nucleus produces serotonin, which is a calming neurotransmitter... As serotonin flows through your brain, you calm down."[19]

Receiving a text message from my partner gives me a serotonin hit in my brain. As a result, I smile and my shoulders soften; I'm left with a warm feeling of love and gratitude for him.

BIDS FOR ATTENTION

You can also strengthen your *We* by doing what John Gottman calls responding to your partner's "bids for attention." Your partner's bids for attention are attempts at creating a connection, and the more responsive you are, the more connected you will feel. Your connection can be nourished in many ways and you have to discover how to do so together. Find out: What do they love? What reaches them? What makes them smile? What helps them to relax and feel safe and secure? Curiosity is your friend.

A bid for attention may appear differently at different times. For instance, a question from your partner can be a bid for attention. Your partner is seeking your opinion, so when they ask you a question, be present and respond.

Ignoring them by making a grunting sound without looking up from your book, cellphone, or the television is dismissive of your partner's bid. Ignoring a bid for attention can result in your partner feeling rejected, unappreciated, or like they don't matter to you.

---

19   Ibid.

Accept the bid and respond in the best way you can. If you are in the middle of doing something, you might say, "One minute, love. I'm finishing up a call and I'll be with you soon." Look up from your phone when they ask you whether you would like a cup of tea, rather than staring down at your screen and saying, "uh huh." However you respond, the important thing is to validate your partner's bid for attention to show you care.

Everyone is wired differently, and for some, their preferred bid may be a bid for physical contact. Your partner might mention that their shoulders are feeling tight—hint, hint, nudge, nudge. This is a bid for touch. In response to this, you might give them a little shoulder rub which will help to relieve their discomfort. Surprise offerings of love and care will not go unnoticed, and these gestures can go a long way to fostering the health of your relationship. You can do these things once a day or many times a day. In terms of making efforts to love and connect with your partner in the way that reaches them—more is more.

What if you prioritize giving your partner more of what they love, and they do the same for you? How would that change your relationship dynamics? Imagine the beautiful flowers that would bloom in your relationship garden.

When the ground of a relationship is solid, you feel stable, and if your partner does something that annoys you, you will be much more likely to let it slide. When your emotional bank account is full, triggering moments or small withdrawals from the account are not usually a big deal. On the flip side, couples who haven't been making these small deposits are more prone to get their hackles up at even the slightest thing. This may include an eye roll, a grumpy sigh, a lack of response, or the fact that your partner forgot to get milk at the grocery store on the way home. At face value, these small annoyances seem insignificant, yet they are magnified because your emotional bank account is running at a deficit and there isn't much give in the system.

Feed your relationship with goodness and it will bear wonderful fruits and be resilient in times of drought. If you don't, the fruits will wither on the vine and you may be headed for trouble. Author John Gray says, "If I seek to fulfill my own needs at the expense of my partner, we are sure to experience unhappiness, resentment, and conflict. The secret of forming a successful relationship is for both partners to win."[20] The possibility here is for a relationship to be a place where both partners feel secure, loved, and supported.

RESPECT AND THE SECURE SYSTEM

Respect is foundational to maintaining a healthy sense of *We*. Without that, your partner will feel less-than or belittled. If you want to have a thriving relationship, build your partner up. See them as the best they can be. Hold the vision that they already are the magnificent soul they are currently becoming. The more we hold our partner in high esteem, the more they will evolve into their best self.

Gary and Tom are a lovely couple who have been together for twenty-eight years and are currently enjoying their third act. Both men are engaged in doing the things they love—Gary finds fulfillment in his photography, while Tom's passion is

---

20 "Men Are from Mars, Women Are from Venus Quotes," Goodreads, accessed January 18, 2020.

playing the piano. They are one of the happiest couples I've met, and their love is a strong transmission of deep care and respect. Gary reflected:

> *"We respect each other. And regardless of what it*
> *is, we have never done anything that relates to the*
> *two of us without agreeing on it, down to choosing*
> *which kind of nail or bolt to use. We ask each other,*
> *'Do we like this kind of bolt or that kind of bolt for*
> *our remodels?' We are in constant dialogue: does*
> *this work for you? Or, what do you think about this,*
> *is it okay? Out of respect, neither one of us would*
> *say, 'I'm doing it whether you like it or not.'"*

Essentially, your job is to love your partner, and to respect and care for them both in public and in private. The good news? Their job is to do the same for you, since you are both committed to living in a safe and secure system. This means you both identify as a member of a couple, rather than solely as individuals.

Being a *We*, or living in a two-person psychological system, is an adjustment for most of us. If you want your relationship to thrive, you need to make some shifts when you enter into a committed relationship. It's good to realize that you are stronger and more capable as a unit than you are alone. You can get more done. Your options open up. You can achieve more when you are a member of a trusted partnership and are on the journey together.

When you both prioritize each other,
then the fun really begins.

Renowned motivational speaker Tony Robbins says, "The number one rule is: my lover comes first. If you're in love, you put their feelings and needs before your own."[21]

Let us return to our story of Jeanne and Bill, who were a tightly knit unit. Their commitment to one another and the respect they showed for each other was crucial to the success of their relationship. Jeanne shared about this with a gentle smile on her face. "Whatever it was, we made our decisions together," Jeanne said. "Nobody had the upper hand. There was a lot of equality and respect in our relationship. One-hundred percent respect. I understood him. I could pick up on his thoughts, and he could sense mine."

Respecting someone doesn't mean you have to agree with them all the time. But it helps to have what the humanistic psychologist Carl Rogers called *unconditional positive regard* for each other. Over six decades of being together, Jeanne and Bill naturally had their differences. One, for example, arose around parenting styles: they argued over how strict to be with their children, and which consequences to implement. They were able to settle on how to raise their children without too much anger or antagonism, and both accepted and supported each other regardless of who said or did what.

Let's review what we talked about in this chapter, beginning with the value of being a *We* and how it serves and supports both partners to feel safe and secure. Growth happens when you feel safe. We saw how Jeanne and Bill created safety and

---

21   The 20 Best Quotes About Relationships by Tony Robbins," on Tony Robbins' official website, accessed January 14, 2020.

looked at how they prioritized one another, were respectful, collaborated in the decision-making process, and did the small things for each other. All of this added up to a long-lasting and healthy relationship. A healthy relationship takes energy, and you may fall short as you work on evolving into better versions of yourselves. Ultimately the hard work is worth it; it culminates in the chance to live a rich and loving life together.

REMEMBER

- If you want to have a great relationship over time, prioritize your partner and they will do the same for you.

- Identify as a We rather than as two separate "me's."

- Tend to your couple bubble in order to maintain a feeling of safety and security in your relationship.

- Do the "small things." The little gestures we make and the way we respond to our partner's "bids for attention" add up, creating a solid ground of being in which your partnership will thrive through storms.

- Create a culture of respect and mutuality and you will be amazed at how deep your love will grow. When you feed your partnership, it gives back.

- Remember the whole, or the We, is greater than the sum of its parts (two me's).

- Have fun loving each other!

THE WE:
REFLECTION AND INTEGRATION WORKSHEET
(IT'S YOUR BOOK, FEEL FREE TO WRITE IN IT.)

I invite you to take a few minutes to write down two things that resonated for you in this chapter. Now, choose one to practice weekly. For the best results, look often at what you've written; your subconscious mind learns through repetition.

_____

_____

_____

_____

_____

_____

_____

_____

_____

_____

CHAPTER 3

COMMITMENT: THE BIG C

"In a relationship, commitment is a choice we make every single day, over and over again. We choose it even when we are tired and overworked and stressed out. We choose it no matter what attractive person crosses our path."

—JOHN AND JULIE GOTTMAN

Let us begin by looking at the dictionary definition of the word commitment: "A commitment is something you are devoted to. It is something or someone including yourself, to whom you promise to dedicate your time and energy."[22]

As I have stated in a previous chapter, your primary relationship is with yourself, and so it's essential to commit to loving and caring for yourself *before* you enter into a relationship. Self-care is foundational to your health and being committed to practices like meditation or exercise—along with honoring the agreements you make with yourself—sets you up for being able to enter into a commitment with another person.

---

22 Vocabulary.com, s.v. "Commitment," accessed April 29, 2020.

Making a romantic commitment means you promise to put your energy and attention toward cultivating your connection with another person. The commitment to being with someone, at least in a monogamous relationship, means you choose to close the doors to your other options in order to give the partnership room to flourish. For some people, however, polyamory is their truest expression. For those who would like more information on this subject, I have included some references in the resources at the back of the book. *Dating* is a different stage of being in a relationship than when you are both *ready to commit*. It takes a lot for most of us to commit to something, let alone to commit to someone fully. Let's face it: people are challenging, especially when you get close to them.

Making a commitment to be with someone can be scary, especially if you have never done it before or if you feel you have repeatedly *failed* at relationships in the past. Almost everyone struggles with commitment because a commitment takes you into the unknown, and there is a kind of *universal disarmament* that occurs as you enter into a relationship. The moment you choose to commit, you are also choosing to not know what will happen—which can feel risky.

You make a choice to go for it, to accept the fact that there is no perfect match and that human beings are imperfect by nature. The sooner you embrace this, the easier it will be for you to commit to being with another imperfect human.

At some point you may meet a person with whom you have mysteriously crossed paths, share common values, a sense of humor, an attraction, whom you respect, and to whom you can easily relate.

When you meet them, be grateful they have appeared. At some point, you may decide to take a courageous leap of faith. Stand firmly with both feet in the center of the commitment circle surrounding the two of you. Feel any fear or the urge to run. I don't know about you, but commitment can make me sweat or want to jump out of my skin. But when you make a commitment to be all in, that's when things really start to happen.

I am not suggesting you commit for life. Not initially, anyway. We each have our own timing for taking the momentous leap of embracing commitment, which I am referring to as "The Big C." In particular, it might feel like a lot for those of you who are a bit older and tend to be commitment-phobic, or who identify as having an avoidant attachment style or as an Island in Stan Tatkin's attachment model.

Committing in increments can work well, especially early on in a relationship.

You might choose to commit to each other for a month or even a few months as a way of exploring what it means to be exclusive with someone. Take it one step at a time. Test the waters as you go, then take another step if it feels right.

My guidance is for you to listen deeply and trust yourself. And for all of you women in your late thirties or early forties, it's best not to rush into anything even if your biological clock is ticking.

You can trust that if you are destined to be a parent, your baby will find you. Mine did at the age of forty-one, and

I had no intention of getting pregnant. Having a child is separate from finding a partner. And when you do make a commitment to being in a relationship, please know that having a child will radically change your life together. The "honeymoon phase" will come to a screeching halt. Best to savor the sweet moments of early coupledom before adding a third person into the mix. I will say I know some very courageous women whose desire to be a mother was so clear and strong that they chose to get pregnant on their own. They were also willing to raise their child alone. In each of these cases, a partner appeared when their child was still young. Anything is possible.

Dr. Christa Santangelo is a dear friend who holds a PhD in psychology, an associate professor at UCSF, and a therapist with thirty years of clinical experience and sixteen years of marriage. She offered this wisdom when we spoke about commitment:

> "Commitment is an internal decision. When you are feeling ambivalent, you tend to engage more in conflict because you are not fully committed. You must mourn the loss of your freedom. Committing fully is an ongoing process. You are constantly being tested and will need to ferret out your trapdoors. Commitment can feel peaceful or terrifying."

Christa's insights point to the benefits of being all in, how ambivalence undermines safety—which leads to heightened tensions—and how being committed brings up our unresolved issues.

Until recently, my pattern was to leave the backdoor ajar so I could escape—just in case. Commitment-phobic? Maybe a little bit. Ambivalence can be seductive because we often desire that which is just out of reach, but having "one foot in and one foot out" is destabilizing. Commitment asks you to close all of the exits, turn toward your fears and your very human partner, and show up.

TAKE CARE OF YOUR INNER CHILD

Commitment is an active process. Given this, I would recommend you take this epic leap only when it feels right. Moving in together or becoming engaged after less than a year of knowing each other is probably not a good idea. It takes at least six months to get to know someone deeply.

Do what makes sense for the two of you. You are making it up as you go along. Be in integrity with yourself and know that your commitment becomes the container which will hold the two of you when things get tough; it creates safety. A commitment fosters trust.

After enough time has passed, your friends and family have vetted your new love, and you decide to go for it, acknowledge any fear or discomfort. Gently hold your inner child's hand. This is the part of you who is scared.

Your fear may come from a younger part that feels like they are lacking in some way. When you choose a partner from a feeling of lack, be it conscious or subconscious, you usually don't make great choices. Oftentimes, you'll continue patterns of not having your needs met in your adult relationships because it's all you have ever known.

How can you change your pattern? Tend to your "inner child." Scoop them up in your arms as you would a toddler and hold them close. Until you feel truly lovable, you will wonder why you keep choosing the same unavailable partners. You might be asking your friends, "Why do I always choose the same type of person over and over? You would think I'd know better by now."

> *Your adult self does know better;*
> *it's the younger place inside that*
> *is making the choices.*

Take the time to do your inner work and assure your younger self there is a calm adult who is steering the ship and you've got their back. Otherwise, these parts will continue to run the show from behind the curtains. Entering into a committed relationship where you feel safe gives you a chance to heal and integrate these younger parts.

Enter in with your eyes open. Relationships have been called crucibles, which are defined as "situations of severe trial, or in which different elements interact, leading to the creation of something new."[23] Something new will be created if you stay the course. Trust me, you will grow.

GO SLOWLY
Commit to what feels doable. Maybe you choose to take baby steps because jumping in for a long stretch feels like too much.

---

23   Dictionary.com, s.v. "Crucible," accessed January 27, 2020.

I made this choice once when I was in a rough patch with my partner and we had signed a lease on a house together. Our doable step was to commit to the relationship for the duration of the lease, and this took some of the pressure off.

If you make too big a commitment, you may get overwhelmed and back out. Or maybe you find yourself coming up with rationalizations as to why it is that you need to leave the relationship. These rationalizations are code for "I need to run away from a chance to grow and to know love more deeply because I am terrified." Your fear makes sense. The question is: do you want it to run your life? My suggestion is to lean in and feel it, rather than run. Fear is finite. I have never met an emotion that lasted forever.

SETTING UP CHECKPOINTS: A RECOMMITMENT PRACTICE

Once you have made a commitment, you may want to set up checkpoints to assess whether the terms of the commitment are still working. Marc and Noelle are an amazing couple who have been together for almost twenty years and have two children. They have a great relationship because they are committed, laugh a lot together, and have a brilliant practice of recommitting freshly to one another on a quarterly basis as long as their vision is still aligned.

Marc is jovial, kind-hearted, and a wonderful mix of wise and goofy. His sense of humor is one of his best qualities, along with his generosity. His work supports their family while Noelle tends to their home and the children. Her soft-spoken tone and deeply grounded strength make her a force to be reckoned with.

Both practice meditation and from the start realized that they wanted to stay current with one another. They created a quarterly ritual to reflect on their commitment, realign their vision of who they are, discern what is true, and recommit to it.

Here is an overview of their ritual practice, which they do on the seasonal changes of the equinoxes and solstices. Marc and Noelle understand that they are a part of the natural world, and that the different seasons affect their inner and outer experience; they inquire into how they can lovingly support each other as partners as these changes unfold. An example might be: school starts back in the fall for their children and changes the pace of life from the lazy days of summer, so they look at how they might support each other during that time.

They reflect on the prior three months and set intentions for the next three. When they reflect, they share about themselves as individuals and as a couple and discuss things regarding their home, their families, their communities, and the world. It's a deeply thoughtful process. They take an honest look to see if it is true for them to recommit.

They put it this way: *"It isn't just a check-in time; it's a commitment time."*

Noelle shared that once the reflection time is complete,"We record all of these things in our big talk book and then forget about them, until the next season, in which we read aloud and notice where we stayed on point, where we forgot, or where life took us in different directions."

This practice supports them in being in integrity with themselves and each other. It insists that they stay current and conscious. They meet every three months and have been doing so for over two decades, which shows their deep dedication. Their relationship works because they bring their authentic presence to it and are willing to do the dance of being in a relationship—even when it's challenging.

BE ALL IN

A commitment creates safety because when you are committed, you know you are all in. Being *all in* even shows up on television. There is a beautiful moment in the Warner Brothers drama *Gilmore Girls* when Luke Danes professes his love for Lorelai Gilmore: "This thing we're doing here—you, me. I'm in. I am all in."[24] His statement makes me go weak in the knees; it's such a relief to hear these words.

And when the eventual challenges arise, your commitment to being together and loving one another is a structure for you to lean into. For instance, if you are at home and suddenly feel tired and like you are going to collapse, you can lean against a wall and you feel safe because you know it's not going to fall down. Similarly, you know that you can count on your partner.

I would like to introduce Danny now. Danny is charismatic, a highly intelligent man who exudes graceful confidence. He has lived in California for most of his adult life, waking at

---

24 Abby Jamison, "20 Love Quotes to Remind You to Stay Together—Even When Times Get Really, Really Tough," *Your Tango*, January 8, 2018.

the crack of dawn as soon as the tickers on Wall Street begin ticking. He retired in his fifties and now does volunteer work and travels.

I asked Danny, "How do you feel about having been so committed to Nancy and staying together all these years?" With a big smile on his face and a warmth radiating from his clear blue eyes he said:

> *"The whole deal is that a relationship doesn't need to be perfect to be good. In the end, here we are. We're in a committed, caring relationship. And, I feel very lucky. I love Nancy more than ever. I regularly tell her that I think she is a beautiful person inside and out. There are so many things I adore about her and I know she loves me too."*

Danny's attitude demonstrates what is possible when you stay the course and remain committed to your partnership, even when things get tough and you feel like quitting. Their relationship is a story of success, passing tests, and resilience. Danny and Nancy have earned a fabulous relationship—though not a "perfect" one, because there is no perfect relationship.

"After all, we're just walking each other home," says Ram Dass the spiritual teacher, psychologist, and author of the classic *Be Here Now.*

We're all on a path and we're going to the same place. Sometimes we walk together for a long while, sometimes for only a short time. What would it be like for you to commit to walking longer with someone than you previously have? Consider how you might grow.

CREATE A SACRED CONTAINER

I would like to share how I am currently growing in my relationship. Although I have done a boatload of inner work, the arrogant idea that *I know better* continues to arise. Thankfully, my partner doesn't usually let me get away with this behavior. He gently points it out and, in the light of this exposure, my *holier than thou* self is transformed. Transformation frees up the energy that has been co-opted by the old habit of being arrogant.

Being exposed in my arrogance is no fun, and the exposure triggers a cut-and-run mechanism which would rather *call it a day.* Instead, because we are committed to our relationship, I slow down, pause, and breathe. I stay put because I see how I am evolving into a more gentle person.

I am choosing to be in relationship with a man who is soft and sweet by nature. If I want to be able to relate to him, I need to soften. I'm learning how to speak to him with a sweet-tempered kindness. For someone who is strong-willed and has been called *really intense* for most of her life, it doesn't come naturally. Nonetheless, I am showing up in a softer way. Why? Because being together is a priority. It's likely that I will continue to be intense. It's my nature. Still, I am honing my ability to respond to my partner with love.

For instance, I am learning to ask him about things rather than tell him. If my daughter wants to have a friend stay over, I ask rather than tell him that her pal will be sleeping over on Saturday night. He feels respected when I ask. When I tell him things or am overly directorial, he either shuts down or gets defensive. In these moments he refers to me as *Mrs. Bossy Pants.* Needless to say, the interaction does not create harmony or a feeling of closeness. When I pause and interrupt my habit of being bossy or assuming, he is receptive and open. There is room for us to grow because we are operating in the safety of an intentional *We.*

> *"Relationship is a spiritual practice because it's a container in which one has to face one's own deepest, darkest side. There is no escaping from oneself. What it provides, outweighs the costs that it extracts, which is an attachment that is lifelong."*

-CHRISTA SANTANGELO

In his latest book *Eight Dates,* John Gottman frames commitment this way: "Commitment is really a verb because it is the actions we take daily to let our partner know we are with them, and that we make decisions with them in mind."[25]

Jen and Jay have been married for forty-eight years, and throughout their relationship they've had many ups and

---

25   Mary Beth George, "What Does Trust and Commitment Look Like in a Relationship?" *The Gottman Institute* (blog), March 6, 2019.

downs. What has kept them together? Mutual commitment. Their relationship has been a quest, full of trials and tribulations. Hailing from Milwaukee, Wisconsin, they were first introduced at a frat party when Jay was in medical school and Jen was training to be a nurse. Jay didn't have a date, so a friend set him up with Jen. It was as if the hand of the universe reached down and put them together through a blind date. I have known Jen for twenty years and she is the kind of woman I would describe as girlishly spunky and "sweet as pie."

They had been dating for about six months when Jay left for an externship in Hawaii, which could have been a deal-breaker. However, Jay wrote to Jen frequently, and they fell in love through old-school snail mail letters. After they had been dating for about a year, Jen became impatient. She knew Jay was "the one" so she told him, "You love me and you know I love you, why don't you just take me home?" Jen's mother was aghast and thought saying this would have turned Jay off, but it didn't. They got engaged and about five months later, they were married.

Jen described their relationship as a "grand experiment." They both grew and changed over time, although not always in the same ways. Both are very loyal, which has been key to helping them stay together through rough patches.

In their early years of marriage, Jen could have exited the relationship and broken her commitment to Jay. At the time, Jen was running the household and raising their three boys mostly on her own while Jay worked eighty hours a week at his medical practice. Jen felt very overwhelmed and spent a lot of time in her head "spinning" in fear. Ultimately, Jen chose to stay with Jay and deepen into their commitment.

Another key was that they were from the generation that was told to "stay put no matter what." That idea is antiquated, and yet there is something to riding the waves even when they seem insurmountable. Being together with someone you love and who loves you is incredibly healing. Weigh your options carefully, especially in your younger years when you have lots of choices. Online dating provides you with virtually infinite possibilities, and you can spend your days *swiping left*. It takes courage and strength to move toward another person, to admit that you need them—not to complete you, but to help lift you up when you are feeling down and keep you from feeling isolated in the world.

The work of Dr. Sue Johnson, clinical psychologist, author of *Hold Me Tight,* and the primary developer of Emotionally Focused Couples and Family Therapy (EFT), confirms that being in a "safe haven" of a committed relationship serves us deeply:

> *"The strongest among us are those who can reach for others. Love is the best survival strategy of all. We all long for a safe haven love relationship. Self-sufficiency is just another word for loneliness. So risk reaching out and fighting for this safe haven. It is the best investment you'll ever make."*[26]

---

26   Sue Johnson, "Ten Tips for a Strong Vibrant Relationship," Ottawa Couple & Family Institute, October 2, 2017.

This may mean that you go public with your commitment, which is a big step. Maybe your partner has met your close friends and you've made the rounds with theirs. You've gone so far as to post it on your Instagram or change your status on Facebook from *it's complicated* to *in a relationship*. You've taken a leap into the vast unknown. You have found the *chutzpah* to stand in the center of the circle with someone you care about deeply. You have grown enough to recognize that nobody is perfect, and you have made a choice.

You are invested in taking care of your partner and helping to create a container of safety and security for the two of you. You've got their back, they have yours. You recognize that commitment is a verb. It means you are taking actions every day to tend to your relationship and your partner is doing the same. You are attentive to what is needed. Your attention is your biggest asset. You are all in! There is mutual respect. You are walking on the path together in a way that is honest, attuned, and conscious. If you are doing all of these things, dear reader, you are committed. Congratulations! And now, the dance begins.

REMEMBER:

- Be courageous and willing as you step into the unknown, amazing journey of a committed relationship.

- Accept the fact that no one is perfect, including you, and appreciate what is good.

- Tend to your relationship every day and do the small things; they make a difference.

- Take care of each other in ways that create safety.

- Announce your relationship status to your friends and family and on social media.

- Incorporate a quarterly check-in time as a couple; recommitting is powerful.

- Cultivate a sacred container and trust and intimacy will deepen with your partner.

- Take the leap and be all in!

COMMITMENT: THE BIG C:
REFLECTION AND INTEGRATION WORKSHEET
(IT'S YOUR BOOK, FEEL FREE TO WRITE IN IT.)

I invite you to take a few minutes to write down two things that resonated for you in this chapter. Now, choose one to practice weekly. For the best results, look often at what you've written; your subconscious mind learns through repetition.

_____

_____

_____

_____

_____

_____

_____

_____

_____

_____

_____

CHAPTER 4

TEAM PLAY

———

"If you want to go fast, go alone. If you want to go far, you need a team."

- JOHN WOODEN

Being on a team is empowering, and a relationship is *a team*. When you are in a relationship, you commit to playing your role on the team. Great teams don't just *happen*. Sometimes you have to put your personal preferences aside for the good of the team. If you are going to play well together, you will want to define which game you're playing and what it means to win. This is where agreements in your relationship become incredibly important.

Over their twenty-three years together, Gabriela and her husband Solomon have developed a deep understanding of what agreements mean to their relationship. Gabriela's buoyant spirit shines like the sun and her light brown skin is as warm as her generous heart. She embodies kindness while being firmly rooted in her reverence for Mother Earth. Solomon, too, is radiant with his gigantic smile, rich dark brown Jamaican-Jewish skin, and an overflowing warm-heartedness.

The alchemical blend of their combined presence enlivens any gathering. When they enter a room, it feels like the air is ablaze with love. They are one of the most incredible husband-and-wife teams I know.

However, early on in their relationship, they were competitive with one another. They competed over who was paying more, doing their vitality-enhancing practices more, who worked harder, and who got more kudos from the world. Frictional moments showed them that being competitive wasn't working. Things changed when they sat down and talked. They practiced *active listening* and passed a "talking stick." In the Native American tradition, a talking stick is held by the person whose turn it is to speak, as others listen quietly without interrupting. They asked each other questions like: "What is the intention for our partnership? What would it mean for us to have a great relationship? What is our collective vision? How can our union serve the greater community?"

They realized that if they deepened their communication, pooled their skills, and worked cooperatively, they would be an incredible team.

Ultimately, they chose to honor one another rather than be competitive, and resolved to welcome each other's input. Gabriela told Solomon, "When you give me feedback, I'll receive it as gold because we're in this together."

MAKE AGREEMENTS

If you're looking to strengthen your relationship, take Gabriela and Solomon's lead and ask yourselves the essential questions.

When you are clear on what is needed, make sure both of you align with the agreement. If either one of you is unsure of why you are saying "yes" to something, it likely won't be long before you break it.

In the beginning, you may not think of your relationship as a team and you might not see the need for agreements. You don't have too much skin in the game. You are two people who have come together to discover what it means to love and be loved. This phase is sweet, but as time passes, stumbling around in the dark can lead to hurt feelings.

Over time you fall more deeply in love; it's natural to become more committed to each other. Your agreements will need to evolve to reflect this new level of commitment and clarify your collective vision. They serve to protect you as well, since you are both clear on expectations and have agreed on what's okay and what's not. For instance, you may want to agree as to how often you want or need to be in touch. This might sound like, "Let's check in once a day and spend at least three nights a week together." Or maybe you agree not to flirt or have long social media exchanges with someone you find attractive. The boundaries you choose will create a sense of safety and strengthen your team; they're about nurturing your connection to each other, which will look different for different couples.

Tending to your connection creates what psychologists Hal and Sidra Stone call "linkage," which is similar to Tatkin's "couple bubble." Linkage is where you feel energetically connected to your partner and can sense them even when apart.

Kathy and Lori's linkage, for example, is palpable. Both of these remarkable women are brilliant, strong, kind, insightful, and hilariously funny. They live and work together and have a young adult son.

They each were previously married to men, and they've been in a relationship with each other for the past thirty-eight years. Once in a diversity workshop, when everyone was asked to describe themselves in three words, Lori found herself saying she was a female, Jewish, cardiosexual. "It means that my sexuality follows my heart," she said. "Heart first, sexuality second." She'd made up the word on the spot.

"When you are solidly in linkage with each other, it all goes much better," Lori told me in our interview. "If the linkage is dented or broken, that's where the trouble comes in. Even when there's chaos at the top of the water, the linkage will hold you from underneath."

It can be easy to break the linkage in social situations. Some couples will go to a party, and as they're walking out one of them says, "I didn't see you all night." This is not the case for Kathy and Lori. If they attend a party, they know that they are there together because of their linkage. "It's energetic," Lori said. "It's a deep practice."

So, notice when you don't feel linkage with your partner, because then it would be a good idea to say something like, "Hey, I'm feeling a little bit distant from you. I'd love to spend some time together and connect."

BEING A GOOD TEAM PLAYER

In my relationship, I am still learning how to be a skillful team player. As we saw with Gabriela and Solomon, team play means not keeping score of who does what. You're on the same team and you trust that although one of you may do more chores around the house while the other earns more money, it'll work out. There are no rules for how the distribution of labor needs to go; the goal is that it feels good for both of you.

Play to your strengths and work together as a team. For instance, in our home, designing structures for practical flow is my domain because I am inherently organized. My partner, on the other hand, used to be a contractor, so when pictures need to be hung or a cabinet is in need of repair, he handles it.

However, if you are the one doing the bulk of the work, something is out of balance. Check to see if you are in integrity with yourself. A healthy relationship is one in which you make choices from a place of self-love rather than from a place of needing to please your partner to get their love; this kind of behavior hedges into the realm of dependency.

When you find yourself in need, feeling weak and desperate for love, check in with yourself because begging is an act of desperation, often accompanied by feelings of unworthiness, and you may anxiously question whether you deserve to be loved. It's helpful to realize that you are a sacred, worthy being who is fully lovable. Know this, so that if any doubts arise you can sink deeper into feeling this inside yourself. Love yourself so much that all of your choices align and reflect this love; allow your choices to arise from there.

Please note that if you are in a relationship with an active addict or someone suffering from a similar problem, you can easily fall into a care-taker role. This is a slippery slope and wanting to be loved at any cost is a hallmark of codependent behavior. If you are in the role of the giver, notice whether your partner is expressing their appreciation or acknowledgement to you. If they are not, speak up. Feeling taken for granted can gnaw away at self-esteem. If you find yourself in a situation like this, you might want to seek wise counsel or attend some CoDA (Co-Dependents Anonymous) support meetings. I will cite some useful resources for navigating this at the end of the book.

In a healthy relationship, there will be a natural flow between giving and receiving. It's similar to the movement of the tides. At high tide, the ocean swallows up the beach; at low tide, the beach is vast, and the ocean appears to be smaller as it recedes into the distance. Allow for tidal flow in your relationship.

BE GRATEFUL AND REFRAIN FROM BEING CRITICAL

The most important lesson you can learn in order to be a better member of your team is be grateful. Gratitude supports the flow of love which sustains a relationship.

Gratitude plays a key role for Jen and Jay in their day-to-day interactions. In their relationship, Jen loves to cook so Jay does the dishes. Jen consistently asks Jay to use hot soapy water and wear his glasses while he washes the dinner dishes. "So that you can see what you are doing," will echo Jen's lilting voice across the kitchen.

When Jay doesn't do what she asks, he doesn't get upset that Jen redoes the dishes; he lets her do her thing. They accept each other, and Jen doesn't get angry about reminding Jay. Over the years, Jen realized that it wasn't worth it to get upset over little things, so she smiles to herself and without saying a word, rewashes them to her satisfaction. Jen thinks, "I'm so grateful that he took the time to wash the dishes in the first place." Jen's loving response has contributed to the longevity of their relationship.

The moral of the story?

*Be grateful for the sweetness and
the greasy dishes.*

-JEN

In my relationship, when my partner leaves coffee grounds strewn across the kitchen counter or dirty socks lying on the floor next to the bed, I do my best not to comment because being irritated doesn't create harmony on our team. Mostly, I choose to wipe the counter off and pick up his dirty socks because I appreciate having him around. Sometimes as I'm picking them up, I'm surprised to find myself thinking, "Dang, how lucky am I to have this wonderful man's smelly socks on my bedroom floor."

Dr. Joe Dispenza, D.C., an international teacher, researcher, and author who helps people to find their potential says,"Where you put your attention is where you put your energy."[27]

27 London Real, "DR JOE DISPENZA - BREAK THE HABIT OF BEING
YOU - Part 1/2," May 8, 2019, video, 46:10.

So, if you want to build a strong team, focus on what's working; what you focus on is what will grow. Show gratitude for who your partner is and for what they do, and let the little stuff go. Keep your expectations around small things low and you might be pleasantly surprised.

We can all be critical at times, but persistent criticism is crushing and shuts us down. For instance, one day I had three out of my four female clients share that their male counterparts had been saying something like, "It seems like I can't get it right, no matter what I do. I just can't please you. Are you scanning for my flaws?" Being critical creates separation and when done repeatedly, often generates resentment.

The first step in changing a pattern is to become aware of it. I often use sensation tracking, which is a process of focusing your attention on what is happening in your body, to pinpoint how these patterns arise.

By practicing sensation tracking, you'll begin to notice what happens in your mind and emotions as well as in your body. This helps you to be able to interrupt your habit patterns as they happen.

Here's a practice to support you. I'd suggest that instead of, say, checking your Instagram feed while you're on the toilet, close your eyes and notice what's happening in your body. You can even set a timer and do it for one minute. Do this practice out loud because when you hear your voice, it keeps you rooted in the present and trains your mind not to wander. For instance, you might say, "I feel my feet on the floor. I notice that there is more weight on my right foot than my left." Stop and feel what's happening. Don't change it or give it meaning. This is a practice of noticing and being with what is arising, rather than changing it.

Sensation tracking makes you aware of your body, and your body brings you into the present. When you track what's happening in your body during a neutral experience, you're building the skills you need to be able to track what's happening in a charged moment of upset with your partner. By engaging in this practice, you hone your ability to slow down, interrupt your habitual reactions, and build new neural pathways which allow you to respond freshly.

If you're feeling an impulse to criticize, try waiting until the waves of emotion have moved through you, take a deep breath, pause, and feel. Deep breaths will help you digest your feelings.

One technique you can use to interrupt your patterns and pivot to a healthy response is something I call *stopping mid-stream*. How do you stop midstream? First, notice if you are feeling tense, or maybe having judgmental thoughts; this is a signal that you are headed down a negative road. Next—and this may be uncomfortable—be willing to *feel* what you're feeling. Turn toward your body with curiosity, notice if it's loose or tight; you may realize that you were gripping your toes or even grinding your teeth; the practice is to pause and notice. Refrain from saying anything until you feel calm. If you can stop yourself as your pattern is arising, you can avoid some seriously gnarly moments.

Let's dwell a moment on the concept of willingness. Willingness is an evolutionary lubricant. Being willing, rather than resistant, allows change to unfold more easily. You will find yourself able to stop what you are doing at any given moment. You can control yourself from blurting something out that you will later regret. When you are willing to do your inner work, you will return to your center and get back into a harmonious flow with your partner more quickly.

That said, stopping midstream takes a lot of internal self-management, and you have to *be willing* to stop doing what doesn't work.

Ultimately, it feels much better to do what works because doing what doesn't work is stressful, and stress-inducing behaviors can actually make us sick. Being able to stop midstream supports your physical and emotional health.

Thanks to my personality, I can be critical, which hasn't worked well in my relationship at all. I am laughing with chagrin to think of how I acted. For instance, one day when my partner watered the plants, instead of saying "thank you," I came up with the next thing I felt he could improve, and said, "You know you could put your energy bar wrapper directly into the trash rather than leaving it for later."

I was in constant teacher mode, which was exhausting for both of us. I consistently ignored the things he *was* doing and focused on what he *wasn't*—rather than appreciating how he was changing his habits to accommodate me. Thankfully, working on this book has helped me begin to shift this pattern.

BE KIND

Refraining from being critical gives you a chance to be kind and appreciate your partner, which creates connection and builds trust. As UCLA multi-championship Coach John Wooden said, "Kindness makes for much better teamwork."[28]

Agreeing to be kind to each other even when you are upset (or especially when you are upset) is useful. Kindness actually diffuses tension and allows us to stay connected even in times of discord. Set up a signal that you and your partner can use to let each other know when one of you has reached your limit and needs to pause. In my relationship, it might look like this: I let out an exasperated sigh, then interrupt my partner with an instant rebuttal of whatever he just said. At this point, it's clear that our conversation is no longer productive and, it's likely that we are not even remotely listening to one another.

When we are at this point, it's time for a pause and we've chosen the word "apple" to signal this. When either of us becomes aware that we are feeling triggered, we say "apple." Apple is code for, "I am feeling upset. I love you. I'm not going anywhere. I just need a few minutes to calm down. I will be back to talk to you when I am feeling settled and ready to have a calm conversation."

In order for the code word "apple" to work, what's needed is for each person to take some space and do whatever it is that calms down them and brings them back to center. In my case, moving my body and being present to what I appreciate about my partner is what helps me to reset, so I go put on music, dance it out, and remember the last time we had a

---

28   Schoultz, "John Wooden Leadership Qualities."

great dance together. Find what works for you. When my partner and I come back together, we come with soft humble hearts; we acknowledge our part in what happened, listen to each other without being defensive, and reflect upon what we could each do differently moving forward. We emerge from this process feeling the satisfaction of resolution.

When we are on a team, we cheer each other on, we believe each person is doing their best, we cooperate, and we offer bushels of kindness. The remarkable Helen Keller said, "Alone we can do so little, together we can do so much."[29]

LET GO OF YOUR AGENDA

Working together and acting with kindness often means surrendering your agenda. Stan Tatkin describes this shift from a one-person system, where the focus is on me, to a two-person system, where the focus is on *We*, as a movement toward maturity and selflessness, because your life is no longer about you; it's about the two of you.[30]

I want to return to the story of Jen and Jay here. For many years, Jen was under the impression that the world revolved around her. About twenty years into the relationship, she had an epiphany and realized she was part of a team.

Her discovery was: "I'm not the center of my universe. I had to let go of me and what I wanted. I had to recognize that

---

29 Deniz Yalim, "88+ Best Teamwork Quotes to Celebrate Collaboration," *BayArt* (blog), September 21, 2019.

30 Goodreads, "We Do Quotes."

there was a *We* and then ask, 'What do *We* need?' It was not about what he wanted or what I needed. It was a combination of the two."

Jen realized that decisions needed to be based on what was best for their team. She showed her commitment to Jay and her devotion to their team by supporting Jay's desire to live in a log house. Jen said, "I had refused to live in a log house until one day I realized that if he wanted one, he could have one. After all, it's time for him to have what he wants." In this instance, Jen wanted Jay's happiness more than she wanted to live in a house of her choosing, so she graciously acquiesced to what was best for their team. In doing so, she showed Jay how much she cared about him. Prioritizing your partner's happiness over your own personal desires demonstrates maturity and shows you've unhooked from your own ego-based desires.

Jay said it beautifully: "I believe that in order to have a good relationship, you have to want for the other person what they want for themselves." For many of us, this is a big shift. It means you do what is needed, even if it also means not getting exactly what you want.

There are times with my partner when I wish he could read my mind, notice what I need, and give it to me. He can't—no one can do that. So, I acknowledge what he *is* giving me. One day, when I was sitting out on our deck overlooking the valley, on a divinely warm May evening, I realized that it is his presence in my life which enabled us to live here. It dawned on me how much I appreciate him. I let this sink in and made room for him to love me in his own way.

Acknowledging what my partner *is* giving me works for me because I am someone who readily asks for what I need. However, if you are a person for whom asking is a challenge, then it's important for you to make sure that you speak up and ask for what you need. There is a delicate balance of receiving and asking and it's for each of us to find out what feels right.

Our team works well because we choose each other, have each other's backs, accept each other's idiosyncrasies, and are slowly learning to laugh at one another's foibles. When you are on a team, you practice together, push each other, cut each other slack, and love each other into the best you can be. When two souls come together, a mysterious alchemy takes place, creating a feeling of immeasurable contentment—a union more precious than gold.

I recommend you be patient with yourself and your partner as you develop these skills. Make a clear game plan. Invest in setting your partner up for success. Their success is the success of your team.

REMEMBER:

- Honor and respect each other.

- Create clear agreements, or it will be a free-for-all.

- Be kind to one another.

- Cheer one another on!

- Contribute your best to the team.

- Be grateful for who your partner is and what they do.

- Refrain from keeping score of who does what; you're in it together.

- Pause when you're upset to interrupt negative spirals, then reset.

- Be intentional; you have to want to stop doing what doesn't work.

- Keep it real and be discerning about what you share and when.

- Work together, act with kindness, and be willing to surrender your agenda.

- Have a positive attitude and contribute your individual energy to the team.

- Be thankful for the happiness that comes from being on a great team.

TEAM PLAY:
REFLECTION AND INTEGRATION WORKSHEET
(IT'S YOUR BOOK, FEEL FREE TO WRITE IN IT.)

I invite you to take a few minutes to write down two things that resonated for you in this chapter. Now, choose one to practice weekly. For the best results, look often at what you've written; your subconscious mind learns through repetition.

_____

_____

_____

_____

_____

_____

_____

_____

_____

_____

CHAPTER 5

LISTENING AND VALIDATION

"When a man can listen to a woman's feelings without getting angry and frustrated, he gives her a wonderful gift. He makes it safe for her to express herself. The more she is able to express herself, the more she feels heard and understood, and the more she is able to give a man the loving trust, acceptance, appreciation, admiration, approval, and encouragement that he needs."

— JOHN GRAY

Listening well creates a connection with your partner because they feel deeply heard and seen. This deep listening registers in their nervous system as a kind of cellular nourishment.

The satisfaction of having someone listen and respond to you fulfills a foundational human need. Rachel Naomi Remen, M.D., puts it this way: "Being safe is about being seen and heard and allowed to be who you are and to speak your truth."[31]

When you feel truly heard, you will naturally be more vulnerable with your partner. Think of a moment when your partner or someone you are close to has responded by saying, "Oh, so what you're saying is that you feel...," and it hits home. You maybe thought to yourself, "Wow, they actually understand me!" You exhale because in the light of being understood, you feel more of your innate wholeness.

According to Carl Nassar, founder of Heart Centered Counseling:

> "When we feel understood, we're more likely to open up and be vulnerable with others. We show them our true selves—flaws and all. In turn, they are more likely to be vulnerable and honest with us. This helps us connect with others on a deeper level, improving the quality of our relationships."[32]

Danny and Nancy's story clearly illustrates how good listening can turn a relationship around in a relatively short amount of time. I have known Danny for forty years, have witnessed firsthand his dedication to his relationship over time, and seen how his commitment to growth has paid off.

---

31 "Rachel Naomi Remen Inspirational Quotes," AZ Quotes, accessed January 21, 2020.

32 Carl Nassar, "The Importance of Feeling Understood," *Heart-Centered Counseling* (blog), December 22, 2016.

GETTING THE HELP YOU NEED

Danny and Nancy are content in their marriage after thirty-one years. However, it was not always this way. Danny knew he wanted to be with Nancy and even when she expressed her doubts, he never wavered. Nancy moved out twice and they lived separately for a few months each time. They were stuck in the same old behavioral loops, repeating unhealthy emotional patterns: this created separation rather than connection. If this sounds familiar to you, take heart—you are not alone.

Communication is a nuanced art, and sometimes it takes a translator to get certain things across. It's very hard to do this kind of interpersonal work on your own. The two of you may need a neutral party to hold the space and offer insightful reflection.

Finding the right therapist was key to repairing Nancy and Danny's relationship. They had attended multiple personal growth workshops and visited several therapists together, to no avail. I suggest you persevere until you find a therapist who fits. It needs to be someone with whom you both feel comfortable; if either party feels the therapist has a bias toward the other, you will not be able to trust them. This kind of healing work necessitates deep trust.

For nearly a decade before the two began going to therapy as a couple, Nancy regularly had individual sessions with a therapist named Jim. Danny thought of Jim as intelligent enough but was unconvinced of the efficacy of Jim's methods, especially since Nancy had been seeing him for so long. At one point, he joked, "Why don't you tell Jim to give us our money back because if you've worked with him for ten years and we still have issues, he's obviously not done his job. He should be paying us!"

Eventually, Danny changed his mind about Jim and agreed to work with him for four individual sessions, and afterward for a series of couples sessions. When the three of them began to meet, Jim was able to get to the root of the issue and help them shift from blaming each other to being able to own their part, take responsibility, and say, "I get it, I didn't handle that right." When each partner takes responsibility, they can each relax, be more open, and discuss the problem at hand.

Danny recognized that their relationship would improve by his learning how to be more present and listen more attentively. Nancy took Jim's insights about their relationship to heart and recognized that for things to work, she would also need to make some communication shifts. It is not about the other person; they are reflecting back at you the things you need to see. After all, they are your own self looking back at you.

AN ACTIVE LISTENING PRACTICE IS MAGIC

In therapy, Danny and Nancy experienced a watershed moment when they realized that they both needed to adopt the practice of active listening.

Prior to this, Danny had exhibited what is considered a classic male behavior (though is, of course, not gender exclusive) of being the "fixer." It is common for some personalities to want to play the role of the fixer in a partnership; they might want to be helpful, and there is a positive intention behind their desire to get the job done. Oftentimes this type of person doesn't even realize when they go into fixing mode—it's the water in which they are swimming. This can cause problems—people want to be heard, rather than fixed. In fact, when my partner gives me unsolicited advice, I'm not completely receptive, since what I need is for him to validate and listen to me.

Danny has a list taped to the inside of his closet to remind him of things he can do to have a harmonious relationship with Nancy. A few of the gems are: "Offer rapt attention. Be self-aware and other-oriented. Say 'yes' first, and then add your opinion."

"Men need to remember that women talk about problems to get close and not necessarily to get solutions," says self-help author John Gray.[33]

It took Danny a while to learn this, but once he got it through his head it made a huge difference in his relationship with Nancy. "I understood that women just want to be heard," he told me. "We began to practice active listening. For example, in the past when Nancy was upset, I would open the mail as she was talking to me or be looking at my phone when what she needed was 100 percent of my attention."

Danny realized he had plenty of opportunities to give Nancy quality time and attention; he just hadn't been aware of them. "If Nancy was telling me something, while she was in the bathtub, I would sit right on the edge of the tub," he said. "Yup. I'd sit up straight, looking at her, and listening intently. I would make eye contact and listen to what she had to say, then I would ask questions."

---

33   Goodreads, "Men Are from Mars, Women Are from Venus Quotes."

Nancy softened in response to Danny's curiosity and active listening. Curiosity is a magic ingredient which you can add to the delicious relationship soup that you are cooking up together.

Being curious is also one of the practices touted by Andrea Taylor-Cummings, who co-founded the Soulmates Academy together with her husband Jon; they both hold PhDs in organizational development. They created a system called *The 4 Habits of All Successful Relationships*, which are as follows:

> *"Be curious, not critical.*
> *Be careful, not crushing.*
> *Ask, don't assume.*
> *Connect, before you correct."*[34]

These four simple habits are learnable skills, if you practice them regularly. As you work on expanding your curiosity—instead of making assumptions about why your partner insists on doing things a certain way—you might gently inquire as to their reasoning. Listen to their answer with a quiet mind and an open heart. You might look into their eyes for thirty seconds or give them an extra-long hug. Taking the time to make a true connection with your partner is relationship gold. And as Drs. Andrea and Jon say, "People go where they feel welcome, but stay where they feel valued."[35]

---

34 Andrea Taylor-Cummings, "The 4 Habits of All Successful Relationships," *The 4 Habits* (blog), accessed January 21, 2020.

35 Elon Gruber, "Synopsis of the TED Talks on 4 Habits of All Successful Relationships," The Counseling & Wellness Center of Wyomissing, October 28, 2919.

Simple skills like these can help you and your partner culti-vate a thriving relationship. Without them, say Andrea and Jon, "You are signing up for a 50:50 chance of surviving let alone thriving."[36]

VALIDATION

In my experience, validation is an essential relationship skill for creating connection.

Validation isn't about whether you agree with what your part-ner is expressing. It's about whether they feel heard. When your partner expresses they are upset, you can say something like "I hear you. Your feelings make sense." This will help your partner relax. It is okay to tell them that their feelings are valid, even if you don't completely understand what's happening for them. You are not being inauthentic; you are being present and kind. Whether they are experiencing sad-ness, frustration, grief, or any other emotion, what they most need from you is to be received with love.

Giving your partner your undivided attention may seem sim-ple, yet it's not easy for many of us. It may be that reflective listening was not taught in your home. Maybe your parents did not even really listen to you at all. For centuries, people have held on to the belief that "children should be seen and not heard." We have come a long way since then. If you were raised in a household where your parents actively listened to you and validated your experience, your family was an exception to the rule.

---

36 Taylor-Cummings, "The 4 Habits of All Successful Relationships."

"It took me years to learn how to listen well," Danny said. "I'd leave myself notes on the bathroom mirror to remind myself of what it is I was supposed to do."

Clark, an older man with whom I was in a relationship nearly five years ago, has a quality of listening and skill in validation that was profoundly healing for me at the time. He is a loving man with a killer sense of humor. An artist extraordinaire, he's also a devoted father to his teenage son. His bright blue green eyes beam from behind his magnetic reading glasses and his smile is to die for. It's no wonder he has been married three times. His third marriage technically lasted for nineteen years, but for twelve of those years, he and his wife were separated and still living together. He and his third wife continued to live together primarily because neither wanted to miss out on spending time with their young son, Jonah.

I would like to tell you about one of the most poignant moments Clark and I shared as a couple. There was a time back when Clark and I were together where I felt totally misunderstood. It was as if each of my body neurotic tendencies had pulled up a chair and joined us at the table. I was hurt and tenderness rose to the surface. Clark was patient. He was humble enough to sit with me and do the hard work of reflecting that *he loved me just as I am,* in exactly the way I needed to hear it. His patience and loving presence were healing medicine for my soul, and the way he listened was a gift for the little girl inside of me who had never been fully heard in the way she had needed. It was a totally new experience for me; it felt like time stopped. I felt fully seen.

Another reason Clark and I were able to handle the rupture successfully is that we took the time to tend to what had happened. That is, as soon as what had gripped me by the throat eased enough for me to speak. It was my courage to be vulnerable combined with Clark's willingness to listen and validate my feelings that transformed a rupture into a loving exchange.

In his book *The Science of Trust*, psychologist John Gottman offers a relationship expert's take on the importance of attuning to your partner during conflict. Essentially, he advises that you speak to your direct experience in a particular situation and how you are feeling; how it's important to use "I" statements like, "I am feeling judged in this moment," and then express your need in a positive way like, "What I need is for you to respect me and let me finish my sentence before you respond."[37]

In the *blueprint for attunement during conflict*, both partners will speak, one at a time. Gottman's guidance for the listener is:

> *"Be aware of your partner's enduring vulnerabilities, and temporarily put your own agenda on the shelf. Remember to be tolerant, because there are always two equally valid realities. The goal of active listening is to understand your partner. Drop your defenses, pause. It is best not to respond right away. Take some time to sense your partner's pain or upset."*[38]

---

37   37 John M. Gottman, The Science of Trust: Emotional Attunement for Couples (New York: W. W. Norton & Company, 2011), p 200.

38   Ibid.

Gottman advises that we "practice empathy," as a way of allowing oneself to see your partner's point of view and validating by completing a sentence like, "I can totally empathize with why you have these feelings and needs, because..."[39]

Clark and Danny both took John Gottman's advice, and it worked.

"I've been in many situations where the communication has broken down because the translation between genders just isn't happening," Clark told me. "I think that as a man you really need to have women tell you what they need to hear."

And he means that literally. He elaborated:

> *"Sometimes women need to hear something out of a man that he's not saying. I thought the best way to get myself to do this was to ask the woman point blank, 'What are the words you need to hear?' If she tells me directly and I say those words exactly back to her with the right tone and inflection, it can be a beautiful healing moment."*

Let us review what has been discussed in this chapter. We looked how Danny and Clark's skillful listening was effective in creating a connection and a space where healing was possible. We also talked about the role of validation and how disarming it can be when you validate your partner's experience—even if you don't totally know what's going on for

---

39   "The Science of Trust Quotes," Goodreads, accessed May 22, 2020.

them. Lastly, we touched upon how tending to a rupture right away transformed what could have been a major disruption into a deeper connection. In the end, it is listening with a quiet mind and an open heart which catalyzes true intimacy.

REMEMBER:
- Prioritize reflective listening. Remember it takes practice.

- Receive what your partner is experiencing. Validate them.

- Attune to one another and to what is needed during conflicts.

- Validate your partner to create a connection.

- Communication is a nuanced art, and sometimes it takes a translator to convey simple things.

- Immediate repair creates connection. Letting too much time pass is a mistake that will create separation.

- Look for ways to create solutions that work for both of you.

LISTENING AND VALIDATION:
REFLECTION AND INTEGRATION WORKSHEET
(IT'S YOUR BOOK, FEEL FREE TO WRITE IN IT.)

I invite you to take a few minutes to write down two things that resonated for you in this chapter. Now, choose one to practice weekly. For the best results, look often at what you've written; your subconscious mind learns through repetition.

_____

_____

_____

_____

_____

_____

_____

_____

_____

_____

_____

CHAPTER 6

APPRECIATION AND WONDER

"There are only two ways to live your life. One is as though nothing is a miracle. The other is as though everything is a miracle."
- ALBERT EINSTEIN

What if everything is a miracle—including your partner? Think about how knowing they are a miracle might change how you relate to them. When you see a full rainbow gracing the sky, doesn't it seem like an untold blessing that has dropped down from the heavens just for you?

It's rare that a rainbow elicits a ho-hum response. A rainbow pretty much never fails to amaze me with its beauty. Your partner is that rainbow, and they grace your world just as you are a rainbow gracing theirs.

What if you were to set a clear intention to build a culture of respect, kindness, and appreciation?

EXPECT NOTHING. APPRECIATE EVERYTHING.

Appreciation is a glue that keeps couples together. There are many ways to show it, and some approaches will register more deeply than others depending on your partner's *love language*. Author, pastor, and human relationship expert Gary Chapman's *The 5 Love Languages* are: words of affirmation, receiving gifts, acts of service, physical touch, and quality time.[40] Figure out your partner's love language and appreciate them in the way they are most able to receive it.

Appreciating someone makes them feel good about their contributions. Your partner needs to know that when they take out the compost or mow the lawn, they are making a difference in your life. When they hear the words "thank you so much," they'll have renewed energy. I know that when my partner says, "Thank you for making this omelet, it's delicious," I am inspired to cook more. He feels cared for; I feel appreciated and loved. This feeds the ground of safety and security in our relationship.

Each of us tends to the other as if we were precious—because we are.

Let's return to Jen and Jay for a moment. Over the course of their relationship they have prioritized expressing their gratitude to one another frequently. It took them a while to understand how necessary this was, and after going through

---

40   "Discover Your Love Language," 5 Love Languages, accessed on June 20, 2020.

a particularly rough patch a few years ago, it was clear they'd begun to take each other for granted. Appreciation was the healing medicine they needed. When the novelty wears off, you are not as excited, which is an invitation to bring increased curiosity and renewed interest to your partner. In the garden of love, gratitude enriches the soil.

Now they consistently thank each other for doing simple things like putting gas into the car or weeding the garden. At this stage of their lives, they don't have set roles like they did when their boys were young. Jay manages the finances because he enjoys it, while Jen keeps the house tidy because she likes creating beauty. They appreciate one another for their contributions, and their collaboration creates ease and flow at home.

"When I feel grateful, I say thank you," Jen said. "In these moments, my heart swells. I feel more in love with him when I thank him for doing something. When he thanks me, my heart swells with love. Gratitude is an open-hearted adventure."

Therapist John Gottman tells us that successful, healthy couples—he calls them "Masters"—literally "scan the social environment for things they can appreciate." They appreciate one another a "minimum of five times each day."[41]

Remember what Jen said about Jay and his greasy dishes? She experienced gratitude for Jay having taken the time to wash them at all, despite him not doing it the way she would

---

41   Carol Adamski, "Living in Gratitude: Appreciation Is Glue for Relationships," *Gratitude Habitat* (blog), October 15, 2016.

have. Appreciating what someone does rather than focusing on what they don't do is common sense, yet we so often point only to where our partner has fallen short.

When you regularly practice gratitude, it changes everything. It becomes who you are.

To paraphrase the famous quote by Greek poet Archilochus—more popularly associated with Bruce Lee—we don't rise to our expectations in challenging times, we instead fall back on our level of practice.[42] Practice being grateful. Gratitude works.

Here is a simple practice to aid in deepening the gratitude you have for your partner. Think about something you appreciated about them in the last twenty-four hours. Now, say it ten times in your head and notice any emotions or physical sensations that may arise. Bonus step: The next time you are with your partner, say it to them and watch what happens.

WONDER

Wonder makes me feel alive; it opens me to a feeling of wholeness where nothing is needed and everything is already given. Approaching my partner in a state of wonder enlivens our relationship and evokes gratitude for his presence, for who he

---

42 Richard Feloni, "Tim Ferriss Lives His Life According to an Ancient Greek Quote That Helps Him Prepare for the Worst," *Business Insider,* December 1, 2017.

is, and everything he does to make our life together sweeter. Being in wonder opens me to a river of grace.

One morning I was listening to a meditation created by one of my colleagues, Sarah Blondin, on the Insight Timer App. Insight Timer is a free app with over 45,000 meditations. In one of Sarah's meditations, she references a tribal story in which questions are a doorway to wonder.

In many shamanic societies, when a person was struggling with depression or intense negativity, they would go to the local shaman for help in much the same way that many of us go to a healer or a therapist. According to the story, the shaman would ask one of these questions:

"When did you stop dancing?

When did you stop singing?

When did you lose touch with wonder?

When did you stop nurturing silence?"[43]

It can be helpful to ask yourself these questions in moments of struggle within your relationship. I find that giving my partner a hard time is a sure sign that I have lost my connection to wonder, and that it's a good time to notice what I appreciate about him.

---

43 Sarah Blondin, "Access Your Inner Source of Hope," on Insight Timer, January 1, 2020, 3:03.

Some experiences inherently invite wonder and awe: when you sit atop a mountain looking out over a vista more beautiful than you can imagine, for example, or when you have the privilege of witnessing a baby being born, or perhaps when you're with someone you love as they leave their body.

What if, when you want to experience wonder while relating to your partner, you pause and see them with fresh eyes? What if, as you sit across from them at breakfast, you slow down to perceive the softness of their eyes or how precious it is to sit quietly drinking coffee together?

The wonder of being together reveals itself in the simple things, when you willingly notice your partner's beauty.

It can be challenging to maintain an attitude of wonder toward your partner during the day-in, day-out experience of ordinary life together. This is where a commitment to being awake truly serves. Feelings of negativity, stagnancy, resentment, and dismay are not your friends. They may appear as such in a given moment because they support your ego in justifying a position. Ultimately, though, when your critical mind takes over, then you are not celebrating or appreciating what *is*. Wonder has vanished.

Kathy's sense of wonder is palpable as she expresses her appreciation for Lori (which, by the way, is totally mutual):

"I like Lori. I don't just love Lori. I love Lori, there's no question about that. Our love is deep and abiding and profound, and it's way beyond what we understood at the very beginning. But there's something else here which is all of those words. It's respect, and that I like who she is. I love her intellect. I love her humor. I love her perspective, I love her kindness. I love the way she relates to people, especially me, but I actually see it in her relationships."

I find that when I wake up in the morning and look over at my partner, his Roman nose standing tall, his brown hair tousled from sleep, his full lips beckoning, long lashes extending from peacefully closed eyes, I smile and marvel at the sweet man sleeping next to me.

Feeling wonder and appreciating his presence makes it easier for me to accept the things that I might otherwise find frustrating or disconcerting. It softens minor annoyances like the fact that when he sleeps, he makes little *poof, poof* sounds as he exhales that wake me up during the night. Appreciation smooths things out.

THE 90/10 RULE

There is an amazing appreciation practice I learned from Mariane Karou, creator of *Dance Alive*. I have found her model very effective both in my own life and in my work with couples. It's called the *90/10 Rule*. When you are practicing the *90/10 Rule*, it means that 90 percent of the time you offer your partner positive reflections or appreciations that are authentic for you.

Appreciate the little things and the big things. Make the effort to thank your partner when they make you a cup of coffee (even if they do it every morning) or when they rub your feet at the end of a long day. Thank them for cleaning the garage and for bringing home Thai food so you don't have to cook. Thank them for going to work and for taking care of you. Look for the good and when you see it, appreciate them.

The other part of the *90/10 Rule* is the 10 percent. This is the percentage delegated to giving your partner suggestions for how they can improve. You may find yourself wanting to give your partner suggestions for how to improve themselves quite a bit more than 10 percent of the time. This, as you might imagine, does not work. It creates a context in which your partner will feel as if they are failing, and no matter how hard they try, they won't get it right.

Over time my fervent and somewhat uncontrollable urge to offer corrections wore on my partner, creating an atmosphere of resentment and separation. And I can tell you, pulling back from 90 percent corrections to 10 percent took practice. I am still working on limiting myself to 10 percent—it's just so tempting to offer corrections. Initially you may need to "fake it 'til you make it." If this practice sounds daunting to you—trust me, I was a seriously tough case and breaking my habit was like prying ancient barnacles off rocks. It takes work, but it is worth it because you will have much more flow in your relationship, which makes it fun.

"The deepest principle of human nature is a craving to be appreciated," said philosopher William James.[44] Seeing your

---

44 Julia Pitt, "The Deepest Principle of Human Nature Is a Craving to Be Appreciated," *The Royal Gazette*, May 7, 2013.

partner with fresh eyes and cultivating your appreciation muscle helps to remind you how wonderful they are and how much you love them. What you appreciate grows.

I know that when I appreciate my partner, he glows. I might say something like, "Wow, love. I can feel how grounded you are when you hug me. It's awesome. Thank you so much for doing your Tai Chi practice." In moments like these, he seems to grow taller and his eyes sparkle.

Appreciation is magical stuff.

Brain science tells us humans are primarily visual animals. So, when you want your partner to feel appreciated, make sure to be face-to-face and look into their eyes; it will register as love.

An appreciation practice is heart-based, so before you offer words of appreciation, take a moment to be present in your heart. You can breathe or put your hand on your heart to help you make this connection. Once you feel present, pause and look into your partner's eyes and tell them three things you appreciate about them. Once you've done that and they have received it, switch roles.

For the best result, do this practice daily to deepen your connection. Beware—this level of connectivity may lead to untold experiences of shared delight.

THE GIFT OF NONVERBAL COMMUNICATION

Keeping wonder alive in a relationship takes energy. In my partnership, one essential thing we do to nourish wonder is dance together. It allows us to connect without words, which can sometimes be limiting. It is easy to have misunderstandings since words mean different things depending on your frame of reference.

Through dance, we open to a shared innocence. It's thrilling to experience the spatial calligraphy we create together as we move. Dancing together evokes wonder, awe, and gratitude for my partner's existence, and how beautiful it feels to dance with him. I love feeling his care when he lifts me on his hip, spins me around, or gently dips me over his knee. When we dance, all separation disappears; what's left is our loving connection.

Now, let's return to Gabriela's twenty-five-year relationship with Solomon. When I asked her how they appreciate one another, she said that being affectionate is one of their favorite ways to appreciate, cherish, and love each other. They share a lot of nonsexual touch, like holding hands, hugs, back rubs, play wrestling on the floor, and looking into each other's eyes with genuine care. The depth and beauty of their sexual communion is profoundly enhanced by the ongoing exchange of affection and nonsexual touch.

Nonsexual touch fills a different need than being sexually intimate. Being sexual engages our passion, sensuality, and animal urges, while opening us to the divine in a way that is electrifying. Both sexual *and* nonsexual touch are important for a relationship to be fulfilling.

Massage is also a great way to connect through nonsexual touch. My partner and I make it a point to trade twenty-minute massages at least three times a week. You don't have to be a professional—it's enough to be present, listen with your hands, and feel love for your partner.

Some coconut oil from your kitchen will do the job. I bought a massage table twenty years ago, and it's been one of the best investments I've ever made. Buy one if you can; your body and your partner will thank you. And don't worry if you can't buy a table, you can massage each other's hands and feet while sitting on the sofa. Just touch each other often.

"Holding your lover tight is the ultimate antidote to stress," says Sue Johnson, psychologist, relationship expert, and author of *Hold Me Tight*. "Cuddle hormones turn off stress hormones! It's better than taking your vitamins."[45]

You will feel fulfilled in your relationship when you do the following: appreciate, appreciate, appreciate, cuddle, play wrestle, and touch and kiss often. Plus, it's fun and feels good to be touched with care and loving presence.

There is tremendous value in appreciation. It is one of our most basic human needs. When you remember that your partner's presence in your life is a miracle, you'll appreciate them more. Spend time doing things that are nourishing and connective like dancing, singing and massage. There is power in the nonverbal realm. When you are grateful, you are happy. Love large, and count your blessings.

---

45   Johnson, "Ten Tips for a Strong Vibrant Relationship."

REMEMBER:

- Be grateful for your partner.

- Appreciate each other five times a day; appreciation is a basic human need.

- Practice the *90/10 Rule*.

- Say "yes" to your partner regularly, it creates flow.

- What you appreciate, appreciates.

- Touch and cuddle often—it goes beyond words.

- Live in wonder. You will find it is a gateway to the divine.

APPRECIATION AND WONDER:
REFLECTION AND INTEGRATION WORKSHEET
(IT'S YOUR BOOK, FEEL FREE TO WRITE IN IT.)

I invite you to take a few minutes to write down two things that resonated for you in this chapter. Now, choose one to practice weekly. For the best results, look often at what you've written; your subconscious mind learns through repetition.

_____

_____

_____

_____

_____

_____

_____

_____

_____

_____

_____

CHAPTER 7

FORGIVENESS

———

"It is not enough to know that love and forgiveness are possible. We have to find ways to bring them to life."

— JACK KORNFIELD

In the vast tapestry of being human, threads of forgiveness and generosity are intimately woven together. They are bonded in love. When we forgive, we free ourselves from the fetters of anger and hurt. We make room for being alive.

In order to free yourself from hurt, you need to move toward it, but moving toward hurt is usually not our first impulse. No one likes to feel pain. When you are courageous enough to open to what doesn't feel good, you shift your way of interacting with the hurt. The pain no longer has power over you, and you can breathe again. Paradoxically, moving toward your own pain allows you to choose love over hurt and freedom over entanglement so your heart can open to loving.

IT STARTS WITH YOU

Since your primary relationship is with yourself, the first person you will need to forgive is you.

Self-forgiveness is an act of radical self-love, and in my experience it can be profoundly healing. When you forgive yourself, you open your heart, set aside your judgments, and leave behind internal arguments about how you could have, should have, or might have done things differently. The reality is, if you could have, you would have. You responded in the best way you were able to in the moment.

Once you are in a place of self-acceptance and have made room for your feelings, turn toward the tender part of you that feels hurt or upset and hold it with love. This is a chance to be kind and compassionate with yourself.

Practicing self-compassion brings you closer to forgiving yourself. Self-forgiveness and self-love or self-soothing open the doorway to freedom. Once you are feeling resourced and calm, you can move toward your partner because you are grounded in your own wholeness.

YOU WILL MAKE MISTAKES

Acceptance plays a pivotal role in forgiveness.

I mean, think about it; mistakes are embedded in all learning. The toddler who is learning to walk falls down a lot before taking those first steps. So, expect to fall down a lot; be kind to yourself when you do. Mistake-making is foundational to growth. Somatic attachment therapist and trauma expert Dr. Diane Poole Heller says:

> *"You're going to make mistakes. It's okay to make mistakes, and there is no way around it. But if you learn to be skillful with repair, you can actually have a stronger relationship after a mistake, because repair is very, very powerful."*[46]

What do mistakes look like? Basically, we make mistakes when we unconsciously blurt things out rather than intentionally pausing. For example, maybe you make an off-hand comment about how beautiful your partner's sister looks in her new dress while neglecting to mention how good your partner looks.

Blurting can often trigger your partner's insecurities or old hurts, sometimes ones you may not be aware of. In a relationship, you need to forgive each other's ignorance. Bring compassionate understanding to each other and be accepting of one another's fallibility and foibles. When you view mistakes through the heart's wise and compassionate eyes, you'll notice your partner is doing their best. They are showing up the best they can, given who they are, where they've come from, and what they are presently dealing with. In a healthy relationship, you agree to forgive each other and to do it as

---

46 Diane Poole Heller, "Strengthen Relationships with Repair," *Dr. Diane Poole Heller* (blog), accessed May 29, 2020.

soon as possible. Waiting only causes your hurts to fester, and forgiveness is the healing salve.

In order to forgive, you need to be bigger than your hurt places. Imagine your relationship is a big circle and the part of you that got hurt is a small circle within the larger one. When you stay present to the larger circle rather than letting the smaller circle of pain eclipse your love for one another, you can forgive. Something bigger is holding you and a deeper, wider field of love opens you to the space of generosity in which forgiveness becomes possible.

"There is no love without forgiveness, and there is no forgiveness without love,"[47] says Bryant H. McGill, who has been recognized by Congress as a Goodwill Ambassador for World Peace.

LET IT GO

When you forgive your partner, you let go. You liberate places within where you felt misunderstood. You learn to let go in service of something deeper.

That's something Danny learned in his marriage with Nancy. Danny used to get upset when Nancy said she would handle a household task or a communication and instead dropped the ball. "I just have to suck it up sometimes and say, forget it, it doesn't matter," Danny told me. "Whatever Nancy has forgotten doesn't matter as much as the relationship does." Sometimes, forgiveness is about knowing your priorities, and

47   "Bryant H. McGill Quotes," BrainyQuote, accessed February 3, 2020.

having the emotional maturity to know when to be quiet. Many times, the things we *don't* say are just as important as what we *do* say.

Let us return once again to Jen and Jay, who appear in quite a few chapters; they have mastered the art of forgiveness and letting go. During the early years of their marriage, Jen told me, when she was home alone with three young boys, she would get stressed out. By the time Jay arrived home from work, Jen would be ramped up and take out her frustration on him. "Back in those days I think we only stayed together because Jay tuned me out," Jen said.

Jay's apparent ignoring of Jen's commentary was in reality an act of generosity. By letting it go, he was forgiving Jen for dumping on him. Jay ignored things Jen had said out of kindness because he saw how exhausted she was after chasing three small boys around all day.

Tuning Jen out was, in fact, a wise thing for Jay to do. Justice Ruth Bader Ginsburg also saw the value in knowing when to tune out in a relationship. When Ginsburg was eighty-six, NPR's Nina Totenberg asked her in an interview, "So what was your secret to a happy marriage? Did you pass on your mother-in-law's secret?"[48]

Ginsburg laughed, and shared the advice she had received on the day she was married. In a private moment, her mother-in-law imparted the secret ingredient to a happy marriage:

---

48 Veronica Stracqualursi, "RBG Was Married for More Than 50 Years. J.Lo Asked Her for Marriage Advice," *CNN,* August 31, 2019.

"It helps sometimes to be a little deaf."[49]

In my relationship, being a little deaf means that my partner and I graciously ignore when the other repeats themselves rather than pointing it out. This creates harmony.

BEING PATIENT

Here is a story from my life about forgiveness and how it invited me to be patient. It was a cold, wet Northern California morning and my partner woke up feeling unsettled. The moment he opened his eyes, I could see the tension pulsing through his face. An incident at work had thrown him for a loop, and old survival fears had surfaced.

We sat talking about his work situation on the soft, forest-green couch in our living room. It was lovely, except he wasn't very present. His anxiety made him unable to maintain eye contact, which I found disconcerting. I cherish strong eye contact, and receiving it elicits a feeling of safety. My body settles when I'm able to have an eye-to-eye, heart-to-heart connection with him. However, that morning he was too anxious to show up in the way I wished he would.

This was an opportunity for me to be patient with him, to be understanding and forgiving. The truth is, sometimes he's incapable of connecting in the way I like. And sometimes I'm incapable of receiving what he has to offer in the way he would like.

---

49   Ibid.

Since I love him, it behooves me to accept him as he is. His upset was an invitation for me to practice patience, acceptance, and generosity—which is not always easy for me. Yet, this is what we do for each other when we are in a relationship. We stretch to become more loving.

Rest assured, neither of you can relate in ways that reach each other, all the time.

As I tended to myself by taking some deep breaths and reminding myself that I am lovable, I relaxed. Eventually, I was able to be forgiving and generous. I was present and gave him all the space he needed to be distracted. I accepted him because my primary desire is to have a great relationship, to do whatever it takes to build a safe container.

WHAT TO DO WHEN THE SHIELDS GO UP

Often when we feel unseen or like we have been stepped on, we shut down. When this happens, it can be easy to go into the mode of withholding love from your partner. Forgiveness short circuits the self-protective mechanism of withholding. Some of us may be more prone to attacking than withdrawing. Both are self-protective strategies. Your partner has trespassed on your heart, which hurts, so you push back and vilify them. You may make them out to be bad and wrong, in order to keep them at what feels like a *safe* distance.

When you shut down, you also close yourself to the wellspring of love that lives and breathes through you. You have not only created separation from your partner—you have erected a wall around your own heart. In my experience, this is painful.

Instead of shutting down and closing your heart, take some time to feel your feelings.

You may need to pull away for a little while to comfort and ground yourself. You might go for a walk around the block to feel the air on your skin. You might do some deep breathing. Comforting and welcoming your feelings may also look like wrapping your arms around yourself and giving yourself a squeeze, or talking to yourself in a kind voice and letting the part that is feeling hurt know that *you're here caring, and that all is well.* Accept the tears that may come. Accept the sounds or body movements that may arise. Experience everything, and remember that your partner loves you. You might also choose to journal at some point.

Eventually, find your way back into the present, and as you do, carry with you the knowledge that you are capable of tending to yourself. It will help you steer clear of black-and-white thinking. One misstep doesn't mean that your partner is no longer safe or trustworthy.

Once you feel calm and ready to reconnect with your partner, approach them gently, use a soft tone that shows you love them, and offer words of forgiveness. The sooner you can forgive, the better. Just as inner untended hurts sink in deeper, so too do untended hurts in your partnership. They stick. They embed themselves in long-term memory and become your default. When this happens, you will start seeing your partner through a negative lens and notice all of the things they are doing wrong, or perceive they aren't treating you well.

Holding on to old hurts will lead to seeing your partner as a threat. Psychologist John Gottman did research in the *Love Lab* over a thirty-year period and determined that when someone sees their partner as a threat, they may experience, "physical symptoms of stress including: sweating, shaking, shortness of breath, states in which it is completely impossible to think clearly about anything at all, much less to resolve a complicated problem with our loved ones."[50]

This is a dangerous place to be. When the terrain of your relationship has become like this, I suggest you enlist outside help from a skilled counselor or therapist. If you notice what's happening in time and invest in your relationship right away, you can turn it around. Taking action would be wise if you want to revitalize and avoid a separation. Of course, it's completely different when the relationship involves abuse. If you are wondering whether your relationship is unhealthy or abusive, I have included some resources at the back of the book to support you.

FORGIVENESS PRACTICES

Traveling through life, we learn that things that serve us take practice, and forgiveness is no exception. If we don't practice what we *want* to do, we will default to conditioned behaviors

---

50   Ellie Lisitsa, "The Love Lab," *The Gottman Institute* (blog), August 1, 2012.

and survival strategies, which enabled us to navigate difficult situations when we were young. As we grow, we discover some of those strategies no longer serve us. Some of my personal favorites include always needing to be right or fighting to get what you want—you know, the usual squatters refusing to vacate your psyche.

When we develop practices that help us eradicate those remnants, we become more conscious, loving, and forgiving. These are all important for our health and for the health of our relationships. Here are a couple of practices to help you develop your forgiveness muscle.

START A GRATITUDE JOURNAL

Gratitude gives rise to generosity and compassion. Some research states that practicing gratitude or keeping a gratitude journal for just five minutes a week will shift how you move through your life.[51]

Every day I write down five things that I am grateful for in my present life and five things that I am already grateful for in my future. I want to thank Dr. Joe Dispenza for this practice of consciously aligning and designing my future. Through practicing his approach and meditations, I have seen how I can shape my personal reality. It feels like magic, but it's not. It's the practice of consciously directing your mind to where you want it to go.

---

51 Kori D. Miller, "14 Health Benefits of Practicing Gratitude According to Science," *Positive Psychology* (blog), April 16, 2020.

For instance, one thing I write on my list every day is that I am deeply grateful to be in an incredible, passionate, thriving partnership. Please feel free to borrow that one! Then I take a moment to summon up the experience of what I am grateful for in my mind and body. What does this partnership that we have grown look like, feel like? I see myself smiling and feel a warm, tingly sensation throughout my body. I breathe easily, and the space around my heart is open and soft. "Gratitude is the ultimate state of receivership,"[52] Dr. Joe tells his workshop participants. By practicing it, I bring my vision into being.

If you are working with a hurt, perhaps as you write, you could envision how it would feel to have already forgiven your partner for a careless comment.

This will speed up the healing process considerably. Dr. Joe Dispenza says, *"When you have a clear intention and an elevated emotion, you create your personality and your personality creates your personal reality."*[53] I invite you to give it a try. Dr. Joe's work combines quantum physics, neuroscience, psychology, and mysticism; it's brilliant and highly effective.

---

52 Dr. Joe Dispenza, "Week-Long Advanced Retreat" (lecture, Santa Fe, New Mexico, February, 2018).

53 Conscious Life, "Dr. Joe Dispenza – 'Your personality creates your personal reality,'" March 27, 2017, video, 3:01. https://www.youtube.com/watch?v=qrozom9CI4Q

HO'OPONOPONO

Another option is to experiment with the traditional Hawaiian forgiveness practice of Ho'oponopono. This ancient practice is a gift from indigenous Hawaiian elders and medicine people; it is imbued with its own power. It is a prayer and by repeating it, you align with its unique vibration—a vibration of profound healing and love.

Start by visualizing your partner. You can do this whether you have wronged them or the reverse. The traditional practice involves directing the following four sentences to your partner by saying them softly to yourself: *"I'm sorry. Please forgive me. Thank you. I love you."*

Repeat these four sentences for fifteen or twenty minutes; let yourself sink in and find your own rhythm as you allow your heart to open. Trust your experience—you may receive a vision or have a felt-sense knowing that something has shifted; this may be a lightness, a subtle joy, or an internal spaciousness not present before. Perhaps you feel more harmony and a loving vibration with your partner. Again, trust your experience.

When you conclude your prayerful practice, I invite you to thank the wise Hawaiian elders who created this practice to use with their people.

Although it may not make sense to your mind to forgive your partner when you feel they've hurt you, if you stay with it, you'll receive valuable insight to help release feelings of hurt or upset. In doing the practice, not only are you healing your relationship, you are healing yourself.

Ultimately, there is only *One* of us here, anyhow. When you forgive the person who cut you off while you were driving, you forgive yourself. Your job is to live in a coherent frequency where you are calm, rather than triggered. Who you are is what you bring to your relationship.

I have had remarkable experiences with these practices. In doing them, obstacles or challenges have fundamentally shifted and what I have noticed is that an open-hearted willingness usually creates a positive outcome. These practices help you to move through things that arise in your relationship—and things *will* arise, even in the most glorious of relationships—so you may as well be able to transform them swiftly.

"Forgiveness is a skill," says David Whyte, inimitable poet and wise soul, "a way of preserving clarity, sanity, and generosity in an individual life, a beautiful way of shaping the mind to a future we want for ourselves..."[54] Whyte eloquently speaks to the way in which forgiveness frees and serves us to live the kind of life we want to live.

Whyte continues by saying:

> "[A]n admittance that if forgiveness comes
> through understanding, and if understanding
> is just a matter of time and application, then we
> might as well begin forgiving right at the begin-
> ning of any drama rather than put ourselves

---

54 David Whyte, *Consolations: The Solace, Nourishment and Underlying Meaning of Everyday Words* (Langley: Many Rivers Press, 2015), 68.

through the full cycle of festering, incapacitation, reluctant healing and eventual blessing."[55]

Whyte makes it utterly clear that we can save ourselves a lot of time and heartache—if we are willing to forgive sooner rather than later.

We have covered a lot of ground, so let us travel back through what we've discovered about forgiveness. It starts with being willing to forgive yourself. Mistakes happen because you are human. Being on the receiving end of your partner's unskillful actions or communications doesn't feel good, and your protective shields may go up. The remedy is to feel your feelings and breathe. Being in a healthy relationship means that you forgive both the big *and* little mistakes. You stop taking things personally, a skill that comes with wisdom.

Forgiveness means you engage your generosity, acceptance, patience, and gratitude muscles. It takes practice. It is an act of love for you and for your partner. Remember, forgiveness transforms painful feelings and frees you up to live in love. It opens up channels for you to connect with your own heart and feel close with your partner. The sooner you forgive, the sooner you return to love.

---

55   Ibid.

REMEMBER:

- Forgiveness begins with forgiving yourself.

- Forgiveness is a necessity in a relationship.

- Recognize that mistakes will happen—you are human.

- Practice forgiveness and it will become a habit.

- When you want to transform pain, offer forgiveness.

- Love the place that is hurt from a place of self-acceptance.

- Instead of closing your heart, feel your feelings; welcome any tears, sounds, or body movements that arise.

- Bring compassionate understanding and accept one another's capacities.

- Use your partner's discontent (or upset) as an opportunity to practice patience and acceptance.

- To forgive, engage your generosity and love muscles.

FORGIVENESS:
REFLECTION AND INTEGRATION WORKSHEET
(IT'S YOUR BOOK, FEEL FREE TO WRITE IN IT.)

I invite you to take a few minutes to write down two things that resonated for you in this chapter. Now, choose one to practice weekly. For the best results, look often at what you've written; your subconscious mind learns through repetition.

_____

_____

_____

_____

_____

_____

_____

_____

_____

_____

_____

CHAPTER 8

VULNERABILITY IN A RELATIONSHIP

———

"We are never so vulnerable as when we love."

-SIGMUND FREUD

The renowned researcher and social scientist Brené Brown defines vulnerability as uncertainty, risk, and emotional exposure.[56] Throughout this chapter, I will expand upon Brown's ideas as we peer behind the curtain of vulnerability, exploring its oceanic depth in the context of intimate relationships.

A PROGRESSIVE REVEAL

Resting deeply in your own wholeness allows you to be vulnerable. In order to be vulnerable with someone else, you need to trust them. Charles Feltman, author of *The Thin Book of*

---

56   Jane Taylor, "Vulnerability Is...," *Habits for Wellbeing* (blog), accessed February 8, 2020.

Trust, defines trust in this way: "Trust is choosing to make something that is important to you vulnerable to the actions of someone else. Distrust is when what I have shared with you is not safe with you."[57]

As you build trust in a relationship, you begin to share more of yourself. In the beginning, you want to show your partner how wonderful you are. The first time the object of your affections comes to visit, you might work to make your home look its best. Perhaps you buy new candles, set fresh flowers on the table, and prepare a wonderful meal.

As we deepen into a relationship, we become more vulnerable. We allow our partner to see our shadows and our unresolved pain; we are not as careful as we were in the beginning.

Love and connection leave space for our imperfections and, as this happens, the gates of vulnerability open.

What is it that prevents us from being vulnerable? In my experience, it is our fears—particularly the fear of being intimately seen. You may feel this more as your relationship progresses because this container becomes a safe place. Early childhood issues often come into play, and insecurities begin to arise. You may find yourself exhibiting childhood behaviors with your partner. If you lean further into your

---

57 "Thin Book of Trust Quotes," Goodreads, accessed April 18, 2020.

vulnerability rather than shying away from it, you will open up opportunities for deeper connection.

Brené Brown defines the elements of trust using the acronym **BRAVING**, which stands for:

"**B**oundaries, **R**eliability, **A**ccountability, **V**ault, **I**ntegrity, **N**on-judgement, and **G**enerosity."[58] Each of these elements stands on its own merit, and I will discuss some of them in-depth and allude to others throughout this chapter.

Let's talk about reliability as an important part of building and maintaining trust, especially in a partnership. Being reliable means you do what you say you are going to do, repeatedly. You need to show up for your partner consistently in order to earn their trust, which means being steady rather than wobbly, like a tall tower of blocks a child has stacked too high.

For instance, suppose you and your partner have agreed to call each other if you are going to be more than a few minutes late. If you say that you will be home for dinner at six o'clock and at 5:55 pm call to say that you're still forty-five minutes away, that's being unreliable. Take responsibility for the fact that you didn't honor your agreement to call. When you communicate in a timely way that you're running late, you demonstrate that you are respectful, reliable, and trustworthy. You may feel like you are in the hot seat. And in my experience, that seat can get pretty dang hot. But being in a

---

58 Joel Key, "BRAVING: Brené Brown's Acronym for Building Trust," *Bloomsoup* (blog), accessed May 25, 2020.

relationship will teach you how to show up consistently with love, integrity, and generosity.

Brené Brown describes the space you hold for private things you and your partner share only with each other as "the vault." Cultivating a space of mutual vulnerability dictates holding what your partner says in confidence. Being clear about this from early on in a relationship helps to build a foundation of mutual trust.

ASKING FOR SUPPORT

When you are feeling vulnerable or overwhelmed, ask for support. It's okay to admit you are not entirely self-sufficient. In the US, we pride ourselves on being independent, but even if you are highly competent and feel like you have it together, you still need others.

Let's return to Gabriela and Solomon. Gabriela shared a beautiful example of how she approached Solomon from a place of tender vulnerability when she was in need. He was working on a project, deadline fast approaching. Before she went to ask Solomon for his support, she took time to soothe herself. She didn't just barge into Solomon's office or project that he would be too busy for her, nor did she come from a place of entitlement. Instead, she asked Solomon for support from an open-hearted place after she had given herself some love.

She knocked gently on his office door, tears streaming down her face, and said, "Hey, I'm really tender and I need your witnessing and support. When you have a moment, I need you to be present with me."

Over their decades together, Solomon has learned the importance of *putting people before things*. His priority was to be there for Gabriela. He stepped away from work and gave her his full attention. This means he came out of his head into his body, turned his attention to his breath, and offered his loving presence to his wife. They have cultivated this way of being with each other over many years, which has strengthened their bond. Take the time to practice this; your relationship is worth it.

Dr. Sue Johnson talks about the quality of emotional responsiveness Gabriela and Solomon share. She has a great acronym to describe it, which you may find helpful. The acronym is: A.R.E. and it suggests the prompt: "Are you there?" She says that these kinds of bonds include **A**ccessibility and warm **R**esponsiveness, as a well as a particular flavor of **E**ngagement.[59]

I know that accessibility and responsiveness make all the difference in my relationship. If I am feeling stressed out around a technical computer issue, I find it incredibly relieving when my partner kindly makes himself available to help. When he responds by hugging me close, and in a soothing tone says, "Don't worry, honey, it'll be fine. I'll come right up and take a look," I feel deeply held; my worries drift away.

Perhaps the scariest thing you can feel is that your partner is going to abandon you. Feeling threatened can trigger emotions like fear or anxiety, and conditioned response patterns often

---

59   Ondina N. Hatvani, "A.R.E. You There? What Is the Secret Ingredient That Makes a Relationship Thrive?" *Ondina Wellness* (blog), accessed May 28, 2020.

accompany them. If this kind of scenario happens, you may feel conflicted because you love this person and want to be supportive of their desire to follow their dreams. However, you want to be included in their dreams. Out of fear that you'll be left behind, you might make a retort like, "Ok, so you are going to move away. That's great. I'm so happy for you," although you don't mean it.

It takes courage to speak from a place of vulnerability, to respond with an above-the-line approach like, "Honey, I feel really afraid when I hear you talk like that. Can you share more with me about your vision? I care about you and I'd appreciate being included in your long-term plans."

GENEROSITY

Generosity is another wonderful way to build trust in your relationship. It may be expressed as anticipatory love and creates intimacy. Be attuned to your partner's needs. If you know they are leaving for work at six in the morning, perhaps you fill their car up with gas the night before. Or when it's almost a hundred degrees out and they have been working at their desk for hours without a break, you bring them a cold glass of water. Anticipating each other's needs serves you both when you bring a scarf for your partner on a long walk after dinner because you know if they're cold, they'll only last a short while. When you approach things with this flavor of generosity, your relationship becomes increasingly more loving and resilient.

HOW MUCH HONESTY IS THE RIGHT AMOUNT?

Let us dive into the conversation of how much to share with your partner versus how much to keep to yourself. How much self-disclosure fosters intimacy? "Honesty isn't just about you telling the truth; it's about how that other person has to live with it," says Belgian psychotherapist and author, Esther Perel.[60]

In a relationship, it can sometimes be kinder *not* to say certain things. This differs from a withhold or a white lie. It invites you to be discerning, and to ask yourself, "Why is it important for me to share this with my partner? How will it serve our relationship?" It is useful to take time to sit with these questions before you blurt things out. Before unburdening yourself, consider how knowing this information may make your partner feel. Sharing everything is not the equivalent of being vulnerable and may not create the depth of intimacy you truly want.

Unburdening yourself of certain thoughts such as, "I'm really attracted to this person I saw at the gym," may mean that your partner can't sleep all night because *they* are now burdened by this knowledge. When you pause to think, before sharing something that may trigger your partner, you are tending to your relationship. Move with the awareness that the two of you function as a *We.*

Remember Jen and Jay? After being together for forty years, they went through a very rocky time, and when they got through it, they realized that they needed to commit to a new level of honesty. Jay told Jen that although he had always loved her, he hadn't liked her for the last seven years! She realized that she hadn't liked him either and told him as

---

60   Jessica Chou, "Is Honesty ALWAYS The Best Policy?," Refinery 29, July 8, 2015.

much. It is common for couples to live together and not like each other anymore. Jen said that it was, "profound to hear the truth from him and that once the cat was out of the bag, it cleared the air."

After passing through this challenging time, they chose to begin again with a vow to maintain a new level of transparency. In their case, a healthy amount of self-disclosure was healing, which is not always the case. Be thoughtful; the heart is tender terrain.

THE GIFT OF YOUR PRESENCE
CANNOT BE UNDERESTIMATED

When your partner gives you their full attention, you know you matter to them. You may feel a sense of calm when you know that you *exist* for your partner, even when you are away from them. You are so deeply connected that in moments when you are together, you share a quality of luminous intimacy and the rest of the world disappears.

If being vulnerable is new for you, this may seem a little overwhelming.

> *Being quietly present with your partner and offering them your undivided attention is enough.*

In time, being present with yourself and your partner will come naturally and the garden of true intimacy will blossom.

"A secure bond is where someone is predictably accessible to us—emotionally and physically for affection, touch and, in romantic relationships, erotic play," writes Dr. Sue Johnson. "We can, most of the time, call and have them turn towards us and give us attention, their presence."[61]

When you offer your full presence to your partner, it lets them know you care about them. I recently had an experience like this where I understood how much I matter to my partner because of how fully present he was with me. We were doing an appreciation practice (yes, I do these practices myself). We began by taking a few minutes to breathe, focus inward, and settle down. It was his turn to share what he appreciated about me, and even though I was not in any distress, I felt vulnerable. I wondered what he would say and thought, "What if he can't come up with anything substantial that he appreciates about me?" It's shocking how my mind can run wild, even after years of meditative practice. My heart was pounding as I waited for him to respond.

A moment later, he looked at me with soft, brown, puppy-dog eyes full of love and slowly said, "I appreciate being here, right now—with *you*." When he said the words "with *you*" my eyes welled up with tears. He'd said exactly what I needed to hear. *Wow*, I thought, *I do matter to him*. His presence and soft tone pierced my heart and a torrent of love came pouring out. In that moment, there was no separation; there was only love.

61 "What Is a Secure Bond?" on Dr. Sue Johnson's official website, accessed February 10, 2020. (page discontinued).

The great poet Walt Whitman wrote," Day by day and night by night, we were together, all else has been forgotten by me."[62]

The practice of being present with each other builds trust in your relationship. It makes space for you to show up authentically, even when you are melting down into an emotional puddle like butter left out in the sun on a hot summer day. You know you are lovable, which is deeply consoling when you feel like a "hot mess."

It's important to be able to be vulnerable and go completely to pieces in front of your partner, knowing they love and accept you as you are without judgment.

THE SEXUAL ARENA IS SUPER VULNERABLE

Being vulnerable means being willing to ask tough questions. If you are feeling like your partner is emotionally or physically unavailable, ask them about it directly. For example, if your partner has become disinterested in sex or intimate play, this is a great opportunity to talk to them. Sex is a touchy subject, and talking about it often renders us vulnerable. It can bring up so much, including feelings of unworthiness, unlovability, and insecurities around body image—to name just a few biggies. Your culture of origin can also influence how open you are with your partner, and "feelings" can get confused with "sexual needs," but a willingness to work and grow together can help you bridge the gap.

---

62   Walt Whitman, *Leaves of Grass* (London: Penguin Books Ltd, 2017), 94.

If your partner doesn't want to have sex, you might unconsciously make this mean something about whether or not they love or desire you. Rejection in this realm can prompt insecurities. Sex is complicated and it can feel vulnerable regardless of your gender identity. The vulnerability can lie in its performance aspect. What if you can't "get it up?" Erectile dysfunction is incredibly common, and there are ways of dealing with it. If you are a post-menopausal, your body may take longer than it once did to show the same signs of arousal. If your partner becomes immediately aroused and wants to engage right away, which might be painful for you, this may cause you to shy away from sex.

Back in my twenties I was prone to yeast infections, which definitely made me want to avoid sex. Who wants to be intimate if it hurts? It was uncomfortable for me to tell my boyfriend at the time what was going on. I was still attracted to him, yet my body was saying "no." When I was younger, it was a stretch to have these conversations. Be honest with yourself and your partner about what's happening, because leaving them in the dark only creates distance and confusion.

It is also very vulnerable to ask for what feels good to you during love-making or sensual touch. It's tricky to interrupt someone who is intending to give you pleasure to let them know that what they are doing doesn't feel good. And yet, in order to have a fulfilling, sexually intimate relationship with your partner, this type of communication is a must.

There is an exercise that is used in circles of people who engage in conscious love-making. It's the art of making a *love sandwich*. It's a wonderful way to be kind and vulnerable while giving input to your partner, so that they can touch you in ways that feel good.

HOW TO MAKE A LOVE SANDWICH

Many of us are concerned that we might ambush an amorous moment by giving our partner feedback. The love sandwich can be used to create a positive feedback loop with your partner, where you can precisely ask for what you need then let them know whether they've fulfilled it. This way you both end up feeling fulfilled and confident that you can respond to your partner's needs in a way that satisfies them. You both end up feeling like you want to come back for more, and the field of intimacy deepens between you.

Before using this during love-making, practice this skill and reflect on how it might benefit you as a couple. Start simply by engaging with nonsexual touch, and perhaps begin by lightly touching a non-primary erogenous zone like your partner's forearm or the nape of their neck.

Begin by letting your partner know what you are experiencing; give them specific details. You might say something like, "I love the softness I feel coming from your hands right now, honey." And then make a clear correction that is easy to do and say something like, "I wonder how it would feel if you softened your fingers even more?" And then thank them, "Ah...that's it. Thank you, my body feels like it's wanting even more of this kind of touch from you. I love how this feels."

That's language from the Northern California conscious dance scene. Use your own words. The idea is to make a delicious love sandwich that will increase your connection and the level of pleasure you share with your partner.

Next, I'll offer another version using a different style: "Ooh baby, I'm diggin' your hands on my body." Here comes the appreciation and your request:" That feels so freakin' good. Can you use more pressure? That'd be so hot." The other slice of bread is the thanks: "Mmmmm, awesome babe. You know just how to touch me."

Bring curiosity to the process. Trust that your partner's intention is to please you, be vulnerable, and share love sandwiches often. The magic of vulnerability helps to secure your bond even further.

A PRACTICE FOR BEING TOGETHER

If you're looking for a place to begin your journey of being together, try sitting silently with your partner for five minutes. Set a timer. Take some deep breaths, close your eyes, and let go of the day. Notice the physical sensations you may be feeling in your hands and feet. If thoughts come, let them go. Notice that you are with your partner, and that they are valuing you by taking this time to be with you. When the timer goes off, gently open your eyes. Turn toward your partner and let the intimacy begin.

Taking some time to drop into your physical body is useful when you want to connect with your partner. The physical sensations you experience happen in real time, which brings you into the present. If you want to experience delightful moments, drop down out of your head and into your body.

If you are someone who has had traumatic experiences, coming into your body may not feel safe. You and your partner will need to move very slowly and with great care if one of you has experienced physical, emotional, or sexual trauma. I will include specific resources for trauma at the end of this book. I suggest you reach out to a good counselor or therapist who specializes in trauma to get the help you need and have the kind of partnership you desire.

Let's review our journey through the intimate and textured landscape of vulnerability. Vulnerability involves taking risks and revealing yourself to your partner. Be caring and mindful as you share. Trust is a necessary component in the dance of intimacy which allows for vulnerability. Take the time to build trust with your partner. You can do this by being there for them consistently in times of need. Putting people before things shows them you are reliable and trustworthy. Own up to it when you flake out, and for best results, do so quickly.

Being authentic and having integrity nourishes the ground of trust. Take the time to practice being together. Bring discernment to self-disclosure. Ask yourself, how much honesty will build the safe container of our relationship? As long as you practice these things, you will encounter the field of deep love where true intimacy is possible. Enjoy the process.

REMEMBER:

- Being vulnerable in a relationship means taking risks.

- Building trust with your partner will open the door to vulnerability and deeper intimacy.

- Hold what your partner shares with you in absolute confidence.

- Show up consistently for your partner in times of need.

- Put people before things.

- Be discerning about how much honesty will serve your partnership.

- Being present with your partner is a great thing to practice; it opens the door to luminous intimacy.

VULNERABILITY IN A RELATIONSHIP:
REFLECTION AND INTEGRATION WORKSHEET
(IT'S YOUR BOOK, FEEL FREE TO WRITE IN IT.)

I invite you to take a few minutes to write down two things that resonated for you in this chapter. Now, choose one to practice weekly. For the best results, look often at what you've written; your subconscious mind learns through repetition.

_____

_____

_____

_____

_____

_____

_____

_____

_____

_____

_____

CHAPTER 9

RUPTURE & REPAIR

___

"Repair attempts are a secret weapon of emotionally intelligent couples."

-JOHN GOTTMAN, PHD

We all have edges. When something your partner says or does touches one of these edges, you may find yourself getting triggered. An intimate relationship is a dance of coming close and moving apart—inevitably, being in a relationship dance will include occasional fights, or *ruptures*, and making up, or *repair*. Issues will arise, and you'll want to discover how to resolve them swiftly, if you want to stay together. When you dig in and find a way to repair, you maintain your connection.

A GOOD CLEAN FIGHT

If you're in a relationship, you *will* get into fights (and by fights, I mean verbal arguments rather than physical fights, which are absolute deal-breakers in my book). These fights or arguments can create ruptures. They may intensify if you live together or have kids because there will be more places where you may disagree. Parenting styles can be a primary cause of arguments; we have so much invested in our kids, and we don't want to screw them up.

What's important is to have clean fights. Pause, breathe, and step out of your survival mechanisms. These may show up as fight, flight, or freeze responses regardless of attachment style. Your upbringing, temperament, and the current state of your relationship might also influence your response. Fight is when you push back, flight is when your primary impulse is to run, and freeze is when you shut down and withdraw. These are nervous system responses and they can take over quickly, so learning to notice them as they arise is extremely helpful.

And then there's our old friend, the pause. In my experience, it's actually hard to overdo it with the pause.

Pausing connects you to wholeness; it enables you to speak with clarity, to name what you feel without blasting your partner. You might say, "I'm really upset about the dismissive way you spoke to me just now. When you talk down to me, it hurts and makes me want to lash out at you. I'm gritting my teeth and trying not to say something I will regret. I am at my limit, honey." You share about your experience, which is what relationship experts Gay and Katie Hendricks call *"the unarguable truth."*[63] It's unarguable because it's your direct experience, and there is no disputing that.

---

63   "Openness to Hearing the Truth," Hendricks Institute, accessed on January 21, 2020.

If your partner shares something about their experience, respect what they're saying and refrain from correcting, or assuming they are confused about what they are feeling.

You might offer the phrase, "I hear that you are upset and your feelings make sense." This is disarming and you will no longer appear as a threat.

It is humbling to watch myself get triggered by something my partner says and go into "fight mode." His trigger response is to flee, which feels like abandonment to me and, wham! We are in a painful dynamic. We are polarized and feeling separate.

Falling into our triggered response patterns is painful and unproductive. All it takes is for me to finish his sentence for him rather than patiently letting him say what he wants to say, which is challenging when he repeats himself or if I can anticipate where he's headed with his thought. Cutting him off is unskillful, and a sure way to cause a minor rupture. When my partner is able to let me how he's feeling rather than pull away, he says, "Honey, I love you, and I don't like that you cut me off; I feel disrespected and I'm really upset."

In my relationship, we practice breaking our patterns and are committed to veering away from destructive dynamics toward creating new, healthier ones. It takes a deep commitment to show up as our mature, loving selves rather than as our younger, hurt selves.

CAUSING A RUPTURE

It's easier than you think to cause a rupture in a relationship. It can be something seemingly as small as a grimace that crosses your face or an eye roll that can make your partner feel dismissed. Facial expressions and gestures can send strong messages, and this is yet another place for you to demonstrate awareness. There is no way around it—being in a healthy relationship is a commitment to being conscious, which includes the little things as well as the more obvious ones.

There was a particular time when I spoke to my partner using a bossy tone and, this may come as a bit of a surprise, he didn't appreciate being bossed around—who does? The intersection of our behaviors caused a rupture. It was a Sunday afternoon and our family was sitting down at the kitchen table to play the card game of *Hearts*—an ironic placement of my bossy tone, wasn't it? He moved to sit down in my usual seat. I called out, "Hey, that's my chair." He got upset and said, "You sound just like your dad." My dad is a loving person but, like most of us, he has his edges and has been known to raise his voice. I did not appreciate being likened to my dad.

This was a moment for me to take a breath, pause, and feel the discomfort of his retort rather than reacting and adding fuel to the fire. It was a choice point. I closed my eyes and did some sensation tracking; I got quiet and noticed what was happening in my body. First came a wave of heat, next my face became flushed, and then there was a clenching in my chest. I breathed.

The power of the breath cannot be overemphasized as an ally for transmuting your feelings. Breath interrupts your programmed response pattern and gives you a chance to reset. "Feelings come and go like clouds in a windy sky," says Buddhist teacher Thich Nhat Hanh. "Conscious breathing is my anchor."[64]

It would have been easier for us to sweep unpleasant feelings away like you might sweep pebbles under the rug when you can't find the dustpan. By sweeping the pebbles under the rug, though, you are ignoring the problem, and the pebbles will poke your feet. Unfelt feelings will poke at you, too. Feelings need to be *felt* and repairs swiftly made; by engaging this practice, your relationship deepens.

In our case, the repair came later that day after we had each taken some time to reflect on what had transpired. By then, we were both calm, available to listen compassionately to one another and reflect on our interaction with neutrality. We each took responsibility for our part and we looked at how we might approach each other more skillfully next time. I realized that I could have gently said, "I'd like to sit in my regular chair, honey. Would that work for you?"

Tone matters. No one likes to be bossed around. If you want to have a loving relationship (which I do), be loving. It's that simple.

My partner realized that instead of snapping at me, he could have named his feelings. Slowing down and bringing awareness to how you relate with your partner shows them that

64   "99 Awesome Quotes About Breathing (Respiratory Therapist Edition)," Respiratory Therapy Zone, accessed May 26, 2020.

you care. Slowing down is critical for emotionally intelligent relating. As Austrian neurologist, psychiatrist, and Holocaust survivor Viktor E. Frankl says:

"Between stimulus and response there is a space. In that space is our power to choose our response. In our response lies our growth and our freedom."[65]

-VIKTOR E. FRANKL

THIRDS

Another cause of ruptures is what is called "thirds." Thirds can be your work, kids, a pet, a best friend, a hobby, or even your phone. They can be anything or anyone that you put before your partner, and which therefore comes between you. Imagine a couple in bed together staring at their iPads rather than engaging with each other, or your beloved pooch who sleeps between you and your partner at night making it harder to snuggle. Thirds arise in every relationship and are not inherently problematic. However, when you choose to prioritize them over the connection with your partner, they can become an issue.

Let's look at the dynamic of how kids become thirds. For a relationship to work, the parents have to be closer to each other than to their child because the parental relationship forms the foundation of the family unit. When the parents'

---

65 "Viktor E. Frankl Quotes," BrainyQuote, accessed December 11, 2019.

relationship becomes unstable, it sends tremors through the family foundation.

When my daughter was born, my relationship with her father was unstable. We went to therapy, did ceremonies, meditative practices, and had long conversations under redwood trees. We made sincere efforts to connect for four years, but we were both fixated on our beautiful daughter—to the detriment of our relationship. Naturally, you must care for your child with the utmost love; however, doing this at the expense of tending to your relationship turns your child into a *third* which breaks trust, creates instability in your family, and ultimately does not serve your child. We tried, but our commitment to each other never completely gelled; we were not a great match, and we were unable to solidify our couple bubble.

TECHNOLOGY-BASED RUPTURES

Let's talk about technology. Sherry Turkle, a Professor of Social Science and Technology at MIT and author of *Alone Together: Why We Expect More from Technology and Less from Each Other*, has a lot to say on this subject. She discusses how being on social media and using technology is making people want more connections with more people, rather than deeper connections with one person.

"These days, insecure in our relationships and anxious about intimacy, we look to technology for ways to be in relationships and protect ourselves from them at the same time," Turkle says.[66]

66 "Sherry Turkle Quotes," Goodreads, accessed May 26, 2020.

Let's take a look at how engaging with technology can negatively impact a relationship if you're not careful. Maybe you've been talking to your partner about the day and, all of a sudden, they are looking at their phone and saying, "I just need to check one thing." Or maybe they tune out of the conversation altogether without communicating. We all know how looking at one thing or checking Facebook or Instagram can have you wandering around in cyberland for hours, which is how technology becomes a *third* in your relationship.

These kinds of distractions can cause arguments or give your partner the feeling you are more interested in your phone than you are in them. I'd recommend having clear agreements around the use of phones at the dinner table, and perhaps certain hours when phones are totally off-limits. Agreements simplify things and cut down on opportunities for conflict.

In our tech-oriented world, some people may imagine they are going to get their intimacy needs met through virtual connection. "Technology proposes itself as the architect of our intimacies," says Sherry Turkle.[67]

Texts are efficient. However, they can be confusing if you use them to communicate emotionally with your partner; it's hard to pick up emotional nuances in a text. You can't see the person or hear their voice. And what kind of intimacies would be derived from a text? "We know that that kind of

---

67 "Alone Together Quotes," Goodreads, accessed June 4, 2020.

communication really sucks for emotional communication," John Gottman says. "It's just terrible."[68]

My recommendation is that you use texting with your partner for quick exchanges, like logistics. The next time your fingers are rapidly firing across your phone keyboard, pause. Once you press send, you cannot take it back. Refraining from "text fights" is one of the cardinal rules I give to all of my clients. Whenever possible, talk, don't text. Keep it simple and have the important conversations in-person.

CREATING A SCENARIO WHERE YOU BOTH WIN

Now, let's move on to repair. I will begin by sharing some research findings from the Gottman Institute. They found that couples who knew how to fight well and make swift repairs often fit into what they called the *5:1 ratio*. And that the difference between what Gottman calls the *"masters"* (happy couples) versus the *"disasters"* (unhappy couples) was that there was five times as much positivity, care, attention, and affection during arguments or fights as there was negativity, criticality, and the other things that go hand in hand with moments of discord.

"When the masters of marriage are talking about something important," Dr. Gottman says, *"they may be arguing, but they are also laughing and teasing and there are signs of affection because they have made emotional connections."*[69]

---

68 "John and Julie Gottman: *Eight Dates: Essential Conversations for a Lifetime of Love,*" interview by Eli Finkel, Family Action Network, March 13, 2019, video, 44:07, March 16, 2019.

69 Kyle Benson, "The Magic Relationship Ratio, According to Science," *The Gottman Institute* (blog), October 4, 2017.

In Gabriela and Solomon's harmonious relationship, there is a lot of affection; they've also realized that there are times when nonverbal communication works best. After many years of being together, they naturally practice the *5:1 ratio.* Sometimes this means making the simple transition from words to silence; other times, they consciously shift from being opponents to being loving allies. It takes time to learn how to do this with your partner and if you stick with it, you'll become one of the *masters.*

DROP THE FIGHT

In order to heal a rupture, you may want to start by dropping the fight. For a relationship to thrive, you need to work together to create positive solutions that work for both of you. If I *"win"* an argument and you *"lose,"* then we both lose. Would you rather prove a point or nourish a loving connection with your partner? "You can be right or you can be happy," says psychologist Gerald Jampolsky.[70] The choice is yours. I suggest being more committed to love than to getting what you want. Commit to loving yourself, your partner, and the other wonderful people in your life.

Gabriela and Solomon have an agreement to apologize to each other when misunderstandings happen, and to quickly hold themselves accountable. They find mutual solutions to challenging situations and when they do, they begin again with a clean slate. They don't hold on to any resentments. For them, dropping the fight is total and it

---

70 "Love Is Letting Go of Fear Quotes," Goodreads, accessed February 11, 2020.

means, "not being sarcastic, not jabbing each other and not grilling each other," while bringing an attitude of tender caring and loving kindness to the shared table of their relationship.

One of the offerings in Gabriela and Solomon's professional repertoire is facilitating equine therapy with corporate leaders. Gabriela told me, "In this practice, businesspeople raise their awareness of how their behavior impacts their employees by working with horses who are highly empathetic." Horses respond well to positive feedback and will avoid bonding with you if you treat them harshly.

The same goes for your partner. During challenging moments, take time to calm down; when you're ready, come back into connection with your partner. This creates space for each of you to self-regulate and re-bond. Although it can be tempting to chew on the same thought over and over, pry yourself away—it's nearly impossible to have a real conversation if you're spinning out. Instead, set a boundary, have a clear communication with your partner, and be done.

PRACTICES FOR REPAIRING THE BOND

The first thing I would suggest doing if you're looking to repair the bond with your partner is to tap into how much you love and appreciate them. See how compassionate and patient you can be. Parenting my thirteen-year-old daughter has taught me to be extremely patient. Sometimes I think about this and tell myself, "*Hey, if you can do it with your daughter, why not with your partner?*"

Practice patience in moments when you are triggered by your partner. Slow way down, notice your breath exit and enter, and feel your feet on the ground. Remember, before a spat becomes a loud argument and creates separation, it will present itself as a nagging ache or an audibly disgruntled sigh.

It's like feeling sand in your bed when you've gone to the beach, even though you've taken a long, hot shower. That feeling is your dharma bell. It's a wakeup call, signaling you to pause and evaluate what's needed.

You might also do an active listening practice to learn how to stop interrupting each other. Set a timer for five minutes. Decide who will talk first. Then say, "I'm going to talk for five minutes while you listen and then we will switch. Will that work for you?"

THE "DO-OVER"

One of the most useful practices I know for both repairing and averting ruptures is what I like to call the "*do-over.*" Yes, it's a do-over just like you would have done in elementary school during a recess game. It's funny how we often return to the simple things that worked for us as kids.

A do-over is when you catch yourself having said something that didn't land well, so you make a course correction. You can actually say, "Hey that was not what I meant to say, how about a do-over?" Then, you rewind the moment and do it over, as if the reactive moment never happened—because if you both let it go, it didn't.

Here is an example of a minor rupture followed by a do-over:

Sandy: "Hey, would you help me make dinner, honey?"

Richard: "Sure, I'll be up soon."

Sandy: (Fifteen minutes later) "Hey Rich, are you coming up or what? I'm famished."

Richard: "Yeah, I'll be up in a minute. I just need to get to a good stopping point."

Sandy: (Thinks to herself) "What is he doing? I'll just make dinner now, alone...again."

Richard: (Strolling in casually) "Hey, I'm coming upstairs now. What can I do?"

Sandy: "Dude, dinner is done and actually, it's overdone thanks to you. What took you so long? It's like you just left me hanging. I feel like I don't matter to you and it makes me wonder if we should even be together."

Richard: "Well if that's how you really feel, then maybe you're right. What are we doing here?"

Ouch. These kinds of interactions are painful. Do-over, anyone?

"Your relationship can survive fights. But what it cannot survive is the loss of safety and security which comes from threatening to leave while you're having a fight."[71]

—STAN TATKIN

The do-over begins the same way although it ends very differently:

Sandy: "Hey, would you help me make dinner, honey?"

Richard: "Sure, I'll be up soon."

Sandy: "Honey, what's happening? I thought you said you'd be up to help make dinner?"

Richard: "I'm sorry, love. I went down the rabbit hole. It's as if I become transfixed by my work and it's hard to pull myself away. The truth is, I actually really need to finish this project. Would you be up for cooking tonight and I'll do the dishes?"

Sandy: "Sure, that sounds good. Thank you for letting me know where you're at; I appreciate your clarity. I'll call you in a bit when dinner's ready, ok?"

Richard: "Ok. Sounds great. Thanks, honey. You're awesome!"

---

71   TEDx Talks, "Relationships are Hard, But Why? | Stan Tatkin | TEDxKC," September 2, 2016, video, 10:13

It doesn't take much to transform a communication that creates separation into something that creates connection. In my experience, it works really well and saves me from having a big mess to clean up. It's like a rip in your sweater. If you sew it up immediately, it's not a problem, but if you let it go, it just gets bigger. Do-overs are a supremely efficient repair strategy. Try one and see for yourself.

"Relationships can survive partners being very different," says Dr. Sue Johnson. "The one thing love can't survive is constant emotional disconnection. Conflict is often less dangerous for your love than distance. So after a fight, put it right. Repair it, heal the rift between you."[72]

THE PRACTICE OF METTA IS SUPREMELY REPARATIVE
Lastly, I would like to suggest a deeply beautiful practice from the Buddhist tradition called *Metta*, or loving-kindness meditation. It has been used traditionally for ages and has an energetic potency of its own. I am grateful to all those who came before us who have practiced *Metta* worldwide. Let us take a few moments to pause and honor the ancient tradition of *Metta* as a way of connecting to its source inside ourselves, which is the heart of love itself. By taking the time to recognize the depth of this traditional prayer, we acknowledge its immense benefit and align with the tens of thousands of people who practice *Metta*.

Metta meditation gracefully supports other awareness practices and can be helpful in the repair process. By reciting

---

72 Johnson, "Ten Tips for a Strong Vibrant Relationship."

certain words and phrases, you generate an infinite warm-hearted feeling. When you do this, your heart can soften and open to your partner. In this way, *Metta* meditation opens the way for true love and connection.

Here are some simple instructions for the practice of Metta meditation, based on *The Issue at Hand* by Gil Fronsdal, a guiding teacher at Insight Meditation Center.[73] Close your eyes. Sit comfortably with a long spine and take a few deep breaths with slow, long, and complete exhalations. Take a few minutes to sense the breath moving through the center of your chest. *Metta* is first practiced toward oneself, since in order to love others, we must first love ourselves. Sit quietly and slowly repeat these phrases: "May I be happy. May I be well. May I be safe. May I be peaceful and free." Feel the meaning of what you're saying. Loving-kindness meditation is about connecting to the power of the words, the emotion behind them, and the clear intention of wishing ourselves and others happiness.

After a few minutes of directing loving-kindness toward yourself, think about your partner (although you can apply this technique to anyone) and slowly direct the same phrases toward them: *"May you be happy. May you be well. May you be safe. May you be peaceful and free."* As you say these phrases, sink into their essential meaning.

Practicing *Metta* includes expanding the offering of loving-kindness to all beings. In this final stage you can say

---

73   Gil Fronsdal, *The Issue at Hand: Essays on Buddhist Mindfulness Practice* (Redwood City: Insight Meditation Center, 2008), 40-43.

the words, "May all beings be happy. May all beings be well. May all beings be safe. May all beings be peaceful and free." Practicing Metta meditation regularly will infuse happiness and joy in your being and a divine sweetness into your relationship.

We have taken a deep ride through the terrain of rupture and repair. Let's recap. You will have challenges in your relationship. Ruptures will happen. The faster you can repair, the better. Be aware and interrupt your triggers; pausing helps with this. Watch out for thirds—the people and things that can get between you and your partner. Offer patience and be present to how much you love your partner; it will soften your heart. Engage Gottman's *5:1 ratio* as much as possible during moments of discord, remembering, "You can be right or you can be happy." Practice loving kindness; it is healing for you and your relationship.

REMEMBER:

- Ruptures happen. Feel your feelings and repair as swiftly as possible.

- Have clean fights and refrain from making threats to leave the relationship.

- Watch out for thirds. They often create separation.

- Use the 5:1 ratio during fights.

- Pause if you are at an impasse and have lost the connection with your partner.

- Practice personal integrity. Self-betrayal can lead to resentment.

- Intentional breath interrupts your programmed response pattern and gives you a chance to reset.

- Think of this often: If you want to have a loving relationship, be loving.

- Engage do-overs as an effective repair strategy; just erase, rewind, and begin again.

- Practice loving kindness meditation to generate more love within yourself and for your partner.

RUPTURE & REPAIR:
REFLECTION AND INTEGRATION WORKSHEET
(IT'S YOUR BOOK, FEEL FREE TO WRITE IN IT.)

I invite you to take a few minutes to write down two things that resonated for you in this chapter. Now, choose one to practice weekly. For the best results, look often at what you've written; your subconscious mind learns through repetition.

_____

_____

_____

_____

_____

_____

_____

_____

_____

_____

CHAPTER 10

HUMOR IS KEY

"A wonderful thing about true laughter is that it just destroys any kind of system of dividing people."

- JOHN CLEESE OF MONTY PYTHON

LAUGHTER: THE MYSTICAL TRANSFORMER

I could not write a book about how to have a thriving relationship without including a chapter on humor. In all of the interviews I did with happy couples, or *masters* as Gottman would call them, laughing together was essential. For instance, Jeanne said, "I'll tell you one thing that made us a really excellent pair—there was humor." Gabriela also shared that she and Solomon laugh a lot together. The simple things create connections in a relationship. Solomon and Gabriela have cultivated their ability to be spontaneous, playful, and lighthearted. Be it valuing uncensored goofiness, laughing at their dogs, or tickling one another to release tension—rather than staying in their heads—they view life through a lens of fun and delight.

HUMOR IS KEY · 163

If you look down the road, can you see yourself with your partner, sitting on your front porch in matching rockers, sipping lemonade, and yucking it up together? If not, would you want to add this to your relationship vision board? Things fall away as our bodies age. When your hair and teeth fall out (hopefully not all of them) and when the gymnastic sex is gone, you can still laugh together. You may even find yourself laughing at the aging process and how translucently crêpe-like your skin has become, or how gravity has invited your once perky body parts to melt softly downward. As long as your mind is still sharp, you can laugh. Perhaps you will laugh with gratitude for having shared one year or twenty years of life together.

Research has shown that laughter nourishes our connections with others, benefitting our physical, mental, and emotional health.[74] Laughter is a kind of holistic medicine. "Laughter can help lower your blood pressure, boost your immune system, trigger the release of endorphins (the body's natural feel-good chemicals), relax your muscles, and prevent heart disease," says Dr. Robin Dunbar, a British anthropologist. "Comedy is better than kale."[75] Maybe this means you take time to watch funny movies together, share silly YouTube videos, and flag those New Yorker cartoons to share with your partner.

---

74 "Laugh It Up: Why Laughing Brings Us Closer Together," PsychAlive, accessed February 14, 2020.

75 Christine Schoenwald, "How Laughter Improves Your Relationship, Because LOLing Is like Taking a Mini Spa Day for Your Emotions," *Bustle*, April 10, 2015.

Many years ago, I visited Osho's ashram in Pune, India. The program included laughing meditation, which sounded fun so I immediately signed up for it. It was held in a big room—about one hundred of us lay face-up on the floor with someone's head resting on our stomachs, our bodies criss-crossed across the large wooden floor. It began with a period of silence which transitioned into the laughing portion of the meditation. One person would burst out laughing, and since laughter is contagious, it quickly rippled through the room.

The sensation of having someone's head on my belly while they were cracking up made me laugh. After over an hour of laughing so hard that it hurt, I had released any tension in my body, and my mind was utterly silent. I was in a state of pure joy. I highly recommend experiencing a laughing meditation if you ever have the chance.

Poet David Whyte writes:

> "Joy is a meeting place, of deep intentionality and
> of self-forgetting, the bodily alchemy of what
> lies inside us in communion with what formerly
> seemed outside, but is now neither...a living
> frontier, a voice speaking between us and the
> world: dance, laughter, affection, skin touching
> skin, singing in the car, music in the kitchen..."[76]

David Whyte's words remind us that laughter is a corridor to joy and a gateway to the divine. So laugh a lot, and let your heart beat in celebration!

---

76   Whyte, *Consolations*, 127.

LAUGHTER IS BONDING

Laughing together creates a connection which nourishes your love, shared intimacy, and friendship. One of the best things about a good friend is that they make you laugh. They might laugh at your jokes, even when they're not all that funny, because they appreciate your efforts. Appreciation builds connection, so if your partner's jokes sound like a five-year-old's potty humor, giggle and know that their silliness is intended to make you smile. Receive what they offer you, rather than focusing on what's lacking, and laugh.

Laughing at your partner's jokes shows kindness and generosity, and relating this way feels good for everyone. When in doubt, be kind.

Most of us are more fun to be around when we are laughing. Laughter is therapeutic and laughing together makes us feel like we are "in it" together. Think of the times you have cracked up with your partner and how it made you feel. Think about those moments where you decided to be a total goofball and came down to breakfast on a Sunday morning dressed in formal wear, pink sunglasses, and a top hat—just because. Even if you're not that outrageous, I bet you do know how to be silly. Making someone smile feels good, especially when it's your pal and life partner.

As Lori spoke about her partnership with Kathy, she said:

> "If you can't laugh with your partner, it's bad. If
> your partner doesn't think you're funny, you're
> doomed. The ability to laugh with each other,

and at each other, is some of the strongest glue for when you get on each other's nerves or make snarky remarks. Laughing until you're crying because you can't stop, that's orgasmic and we have laughing orgasms together."

Laughing together and sharing private jokes bonds you as a couple. Over time, you will collect a sack full of hilariously funny things that happened when you were together, things that made you laugh until tears ran down your face and you felt like you were going to pee in your pants. As time passes, you may begin to share a kind of a secret language. It's a private language composed of inside jokes. Eventually, these can be reduced to a word, a phrase, or a nearly imperceptible gesture (the kind you would only notice if you were privy to the joke). Like when someone makes a joke, and you don't get it and they say, "You had to be there."

Remember Clark? He is one of my ex-partners and is definitely one of the funniest people I've ever known. He laughs a lot, and the sound of his chuckle warms a room like a crackling fire. Humor is a requirement in his life, and he leans on it in a variety of situations.

"In a relationship, I would say that it's not just humor, but a compatible sense of humor that really makes something work," Clark told me. "If you have a common understanding of irony with your partner, you're speaking the same language." Sharing a common language enables you to play together on the far edges of reality, which is a lot fun!

It is a bit like what Dr. Seuss once said:

"People are weird. When we find someone with weirdness compatible with ours, we team up and call it love."[77]

-DR. SEUSS

We love one another more fully when we "get" each other, and getting each other's humor lubricates our systems and creates flow. My partner and I have shared some awesome moments of laughing together over nothing. We love to create acronyms and linguistically riff together (LRT), invent new words, and just enjoy being silly.

HUMOR IS A SALVE DURING CONFLICT

"Laughter helps heal rifts or disagreements. It really takes the edge off," write researchers at Newport Academy. "Specifically, laughing with your partner helps you take yourself less seriously. As a result, we become less defensive and less stuck in our own point of view."[78]

Here is an example of a relationship where humor has been healing. Let me introduce Tom and Andrea. Humor has been

---

77 Cassandra Neace, "25 Dr. Seuss Quotes to Remind You to Be Good and Do Good," *Book Riot*, July 30, 2018.

78 "Why Laughter Is Good for Mental Health," Newport Academy (website), March 30, 2018.

their ally throughout their fifty-three year long relationship. They met when they were eighteen; they both turned seventy-five this year and are family and community elders. Tom is a psychotherapist, published author, and a Huichol-trained shaman while Andrea worked as a registered pediatric nurse and a midwife for thirty years.

Tom has led vision quests for forty years, which demonstrates his commitment to inquiry. His beloved wife Andrea is a strong, warm-hearted woman with sunbaked skin and bright eyes.

I began my interview with Tom and Andrea by asking, "What has made your relationship work?" Instantly, their penchant for relentless banter appeared.

"I think the main fact is that I haven't presented any tests for Andrea at all," Tom said with a wink and a belly laugh. He was referring to a moment in their garden as he looked at Andrea and said, "I have a more pleasant personality than I used to, don't I?" Joking around has helped Tom and Andrea get through some rough moments. Back when they were newlyweds and had two young daughters vying for their attention, they fought. Eventually, one of them would say, "If this is so hard, why don't you move out?" They would go back and forth: "No, you move out." "I don't want to move out, you move out."

It didn't take long for them to realize how absurd they were being, stop fighting, and start laughing. "The funny part of that story was that neither of us had the money to pay for another place to live," Tom said. Then they both burst out laughing at how reactive they were back then. Laughter was a healing salve for these two healers.

Our old friends Jen and Jay have also leaned on laughter during some tough moments. Jen told me that sometimes when they argued, it would get loud. Once they realized how ridiculous they were being, they would laugh at themselves for getting so worked up and the tension between them would dissolve like sugar in a hot cup of tea.

"Laughter is really the key to what has kept us together," Jen says. "We have learned to laugh at ourselves, each other and the kids. Jay has a great sense of humor which I appreciate and I make him laugh too. It works well for us."

A word to the wise: misplaced humor can backfire and exacerbate a conflict. Make sure you are laughing with rather than at your partner. It's also important to take care not to overuse humor because it can easily turn into sarcasm or excessive criticism.

In my experience, it is useful to pause before saying anything that could be perceived as a threat. Joking around can easily go too far and become dangerous for your relationship.

In one study, psychologist Robert W. Levenson of the University of California at Berkeley asked couples to discuss something about their partner that annoyed them.

"Subsequently, some couples laughed and smiled while having the conversation," reads the study. "As a result, they not only felt better immediately, but also reported higher levels of satisfaction in their relationship. Furthermore, Levenson found that these couples stayed together longer."[79]

The moral of the story? People who have happy, long-term relationships laugh together—a lot!

LAUGHTER IN THE BEDROOM

Let's talk about sex and its relationship to laughter. Being present is what, in my experience, makes for the best sex ever, and laughter opens you to presence. Sexual intimacy happens when you are turned on, and in order to really connect you need to relax and let yourself be vulnerable—vulnerability is sexy. In these moments, laughter must be well-placed, or it may be misinterpreted.

The sexual arena is highly delicate, and laughing together about embarrassing things that happen creates a connection, a sense of safety, and helps to soften awkward moments. When my partner and I talk about love-making, we try not to make a strange moment mean anything about how we feel about each other, especially when something uncomfortable happens, like dwindling passion or when one of us is spacing out, because it happens.

Laughter can soften the awkwardness that can happen while you are in the act—like in the case of burps, or farts, or even what are known as "queefs" (vaginal farts), all of which can sometimes be startlingly loud. The body does all kinds of wild things and many can happen while you are having sex,

---

79 Ibid.

and not only during vaginal intercourse. Have you ever had your partner's sweat dripping all over you or experienced a drop of their saltiness falling and landing right in your eye? I have, and it can be pretty funny. If you prefer the athletic variety of love-making, you might find yourself in yoga poses like plank or straddle splits.

And for all of you who have experienced female ejaculation and created a puddle on the bed, you know laughing helps to avoid feeling massively embarrassed. Likewise, you might feel embarrassed if you ejaculate prematurely or simply can't "get it up." Just so you know, these moments are not at all uncommon. Levity can be helpful.

It is common to romanticize what sex will be like with a new partner, and you may have all kinds of ideas about how it *should* be (we have Hollywood to thank for this). However, *shoulds* are incredibly limiting and they are the bedfellows (no pun intended) of judgement. Judgement has no place in the bedroom. If you want to snuff out a romantic flame, judgement will do it every time. Drop all of your preconceived notions and be present.

Sexuality can be expressed in a zillion different ways—from tender to wild, routine or creative, relaxed, prayerful, acrobatic, sweet, or nourishing.

Regardless, the possibility in being sexually intimate is for you to feel connected with yourself, your partner, and in the best-case scenario, with the divine. True love-making can be very healing and even evolutionary.

Laugher—the glue that can enhance sexual experiences and can turn fights into bonding moments—is healing for a relationship in many ways, so do it together, and do it often. Laughter can act as a salve during moments of conflict. It serves as an ally, and during fights it can help you to interrupt your patterns and see how silly you both are being, or reveal how you've gotten pulled into a negative spiral by something ultimately inconsequential.

REMEMBER:

- Laugh together to deepen your connection with your partner.

- If you want to pull yourselves out of a conflict, laughter can be the best medicine.

- Join the happy couples club and make laughing with your partner a priority. Remember, comedy is better than kale.

- Make jokes regularly, but don't overdo it. Humor loses its potency when overused.

- Laugh together in the bedroom; you will have more fun and laughing will dissipate awkwardness. Everyone farts sometimes during sex. Let it go and laugh about it.

HUMOR IS KEY:
REFLECTION AND INTEGRATION WORKSHEET
(IT'S YOUR BOOK, FEEL FREE TO WRITE IN IT.)

I invite you to take a few minutes to write down two things that resonated for you in this chapter. Now, choose one to practice weekly. For the best results, look often at what you've written; your subconscious mind learns through repetition.

_____

_____

_____

_____

_____

_____

_____

_____

_____

_____

_____

CHAPTER 11

UNCONDITIONAL ACCEPTANCE

———

"I've learned that people will forget what you said, people will forget what you did, but people will never forget how you made them feel."

-CARL W. BUEHNER

One of the most important things you can offer your partner is unconditional acceptance, which is a big ask. To engage in unconditionality insists we go beyond our ego and offer a level of generosity not found in the ego's repertoire. Unconditionality invites us to be bigger than our individual needs and desires, and the alignment with our infinitely vast self enables us to accept our partner as they are.

Safety is primary. It allows us to open and reveal ourselves to another person, which in turn makes us available to the intimate dance of loving. As therapist and author David Richo clearly states, "Acceptance is unconditional since it means validating someone's choices and lifestyle even when we do not agree with them."[80] You have to accept your partner as they are, rather than wanting them to be different. Unconditional acceptance is an offering which we must first make to ourselves and then to one another.

ATTUNING TO YOUR PARTNER'S NEEDS

Attuning means taking the time to notice how your partner is feeling and listen closely to what they are saying or not saying. For clarity, what I am offering is that you *attune* to your partner rather than reading into them: be curious and ask questions rather than assuming, and speak up from a place of personal integrity rather than make demands. Attuning is an art and your task is to *grok,* or intuitively and profoundly understand your partner.[81]

Learning to *grok* your partner is a rich and unending endeavor.

"You can spend a lifetime being curious about the inner world of your partner, and being brave enough to share your own inner world, and never be done discovering all there is to know about each other." "It's exciting."[82]

- JOHN GOTTMAN

80 David Richo, *How to Be an Adult in Relationships* (Boston: Shambala Publications, 2002), 32.

81 *Merriam-Webster,* s.v. "Grok (v.)," accessed February 16, 2020.

82 Goodreads, "Eight Dates Quotes."

As you and your partner discover each other's inner worlds, you'll find yourselves back in the conversation about attachment styles and needs.

Based on attachment styles, your individual needs for space and connection can vary. It is useful to accept your partner's need for space instead of taking it personally; acceptance creates a harmonious tenor in your relationship. Pay close attention when, rather than communicating with words, they demonstrate their need for personal space through actions like physically pulling away. In moments like these, you can trust they have hit their capacity for emotional intimacy.

If your partner is more of a "shower" than a talker, as many Islands tend to be, you may find studying your partner, a great thing for both of you to do regardless of attachment style, helps you to learn to read even their most subtle signals. Studying your partner means setting your own agenda aside and instead being curious.

Along your relationship journey, you may discover not everyone knows what they need in the moment they need it. Some people need more time to know what they are feeling than others. For instance, you may have a partner who shuts down rather than continuing to engage with you when they are "full," or have reached their capacity for relating. Don't take this personally. If you get upset, you'll likely say something you will regret—sending your partner even deeper into their shell. Instead, what if you were able to witness their withdrawal with compassion while remaining calm?

In my experience, this makes it easier to understand why sometimes my partner chooses not to come upstairs to hug or kiss me goodbye. When my partner is full, he calls out" ,Bye honey, see you later," without giving me a squeeze. Why? Because that's the level of intimacy he can handle in the moment. When this happens with my partner, I tend to myself with care if his actions have left me to face my fear of being abandoned; this may also apply to you if you have Wave tendencies.

People have very different intimacy needs. It can be challenging when you discover your partner's needs are at the other end of the spectrum from your own. You may be someone who feels happier being connected all the time—be it through hanging out, checking in on the phone, or sending texts back and forth all day long. If this need for constant connection describes you, you are probably in the Wave category. Generally speaking, Waves place a high value on connection. It helps to reassure them they will not be abandoned, which allows their nervous systems to relax.

Next, let us revisit the Island, which is another flavor of insecure attachment. As I described in the first chapter, Islands grew up spending a lot of time alone and taking care of themselves, maybe even to the point of being neglected. A paltry amount of attention is what feels comfortable to them and they will not be inclined to text you multiple times a day, or be in close physical proximity 24/7. They may enjoy physical contact, but only so much. It's unlikely they would receive a nickname like "The Clingster." They need their space and tend to feel easily encroached upon. Islands may have had a caregiver who overstepped their personal boundaries or neglected them in some way, and they may have learned to protect themselves by going inward and keeping their feelings inside. When you relate to an Island, you may need to do some detective work to piece together what they are actually saying.

In my own relationship, I find my need for connection is generally higher than my partner's. When he was away at his office, it felt to me like he was no longer on the planet—my experience was one of total radio silence. I realized it wasn't working for me not to hear a peep from him all day. I knew he took breaks during his day to go for walks or play ping-pong with his colleagues. I wondered why he didn't think to reach out to me during his walk. When I asked him about this, his response was, "I hadn't thought about it. I just like to walk and feel the sun on my face."

We talked about it and I gently said, "Love, I would really appreciate it if you would reach out to me once a day because when you do, I feel connected to you." When he began texting or calling me each afternoon (he set a reminder on his calendar to not forget), the feeling of being disconnected went away. It was an easy ask for me and a simple fix for him. Our daily communication ritual addressed the deeper issue of our different connection needs.

Before making any requests, I took some time to feel my feelings and accept that his lack of contact was not about me or his feelings for me. By taking care of myself, I was able to accept that his minimal communication was due to the level of focus he needs to maintain at work. He also hadn't realized more frequent communication would have such a strong positive effect on me. It helped that I was able to keep my heart open and make a clear request rather than using blaming language like, "Wow, you really don't care about me enough to send me one text during the whole day?"—which may have led him to believe that he had done something wrong.

> *Emotionally intelligent communication helps to avoid causing ruptures in your relationship.*

A great way to tend to the container of your relationship is not to take things personally—this opens you to experiencing real freedom. This is freedom from identification with the ego, which is at the root of suffering. Be aware of the meaning you give to things and notice if you are falling into a "this means that" way of thinking. Trust me, most of the time, it's not about you.

GETTING YOUR NEEDS MET—OR NOT

It's important to accept that no matter how strong your relationship is, your partner will never meet all of your needs. "Mature adults seek only about 25 percent of their need fulfillment from someone else," writes psychotherapist David Richo, "and the rest from friends, community, career, spirituality and even pets..."[83]

---

83   Richo, *How to Be an Adult in Relationships*, 70-71.

It's best not to try to get 100 percent of your needs met by your partner; you are setting yourself up for disappointment. No one person can provide everything—that's where friends, communities, and dogs come in.

Babies are a different story. From the time we are in utero, the contract between mother and child is that the mother will sustain the child; she gives the fetus physical nourishment to grow.

Since this relationship is our earliest imprint of what it means to be in a relationship, this also points to why we later seek a secure dyadic connection with one person. All our relationships remind us of our first relationship, the one we had with our mother. It's as if we are trying to get back to that feeling of being taken care of. We are searching for a place to rest where we feel *at home*. In a healthy partnership, you will feel at home—that said, your true home lies within your own heart. The experience of both being at home in yourself and in your relationship is profoundly nourishing.

GIVING SPACE

Sometimes being at home in your partnership means learning to be independent. For example, in Jen's life with Jay, she said, "I had to learn that I needed to do what I wanted to do, regardless of whether Jay joined me or not. I think I learned this halfway through our relationship (about twenty-five years in), that I needed to listen to my heart and fulfill my own needs."

Early on in a relationship, we tend to want to merge with our newfound love. Merging contributes to bonding and, eventually, we need to individuate, to find balance, and learn independence—all of which can be quite freeing. When you accept that you and your partner will not always want to do the same thing, or eat the same food, it takes the pressure off. You can still be united in *We*-ness while honoring your individual needs and personal preferences.

My partner tends toward vegetarianism, while I eat poultry and fish. We accept this and it's not a big deal for us to eat different meals because we respect each other and accept our differences. Aspects of acceptance range between physical, emotional, and spiritual. You can be very different from your partner and have a thriving relationship, as long as you accept one another and are willing to do your own inner work when you find yourself challenged by your differences. Unconditional acceptance means you choose your partner again and again.

Let's go back to Jen and Jay. They found doing things on their own during the latter stage of their relationship was crucial. Jen realized this when she'd ask Jay things like, "Would you like to join me for a concert on Friday night?" and he'd unenthusiastically respond, "Ok, if you want to go, I'll go." Jen didn't appreciate his lack of enthusiasm and decided she would rather attend a concert or a film alone than feel like she was dragging along a heavy sack of potatoes. Jay agreed, and each wanted the other to be happy, even if it meant taking separate vacations (which they often did).

One of Jay's passions is scuba diving, yet Jen does not enjoy it. So he travels to Hawaii or the Maldives to dive on his own. Jen loves meditation retreats; Jay stays at home since it is not his thing. Supporting your partner to do what fills them up helps them to feel accepted and loved.

You need to discover how much space you and your partner each need. There are many couples for whom spending the majority of their time together works well and in fifty years together, they may have never even considered taking separate vacations. Honor what works for you as a couple, even when it goes against what society dictates. Find a rhythm of spending time—together and apart—that meets both of your needs.

Accepting your partner and giving them space may look like navigating between being an ally who makes suggestions and an observer who lets them find their way. Be respectful and refrain from interfering with their process. You can empower them to find their own solutions, rather than offering unsolicited advice. We are like butterflies who must pump their wings to emerge from the chrysalis if we want to be able to fly.

For instance, if your partner is struggling with their weight, or not taking good care of their health, you would do well to let them find their own way. Of course, you can be supportive by preparing healthy meals and green smoothies, but you cannot do their work for them. Self-care is based in self-love and self-respect. You can't rush your partner's journey into self-love or ask them to hurry up and evolve. Giving space and accepting your partner asks you to practice a lot of internal self-management, as you stand back and watch them do things that may not be in their best interest. Unless what they are doing or not doing is dangerous, you'd be wise to back off and let them be, just as you would want them to do for you.

Accept your partner in all of their neuroses.
We all have them.

Everyone can become a little (or a lot) *unglued* sometimes. "The point is that neuroses don't have to ruin a marriage (relationship)," John Gottman writes. "If you can accommodate each other's 'crazy' side and handle it with caring, affection, and respect, your [relationship] can thrive."[84] He is speaking to the generous flavor of acceptance you can offer your partner. This includes accepting when your partner is feeling sad, unworthy, or depressed. Being in a relationship means being in for *all* of it which means you stick together—happy or sad.

TALK ABOUT IT
Whatever your needs may be around giving or taking space, it is important to talk about them. Taking space without communicating can easily be misconstrued. I suggest you have a mindful conversation (which does not necessitate massive amounts of processing; beware, over-processing can also drag a relationship into the mud). Be present and notice your breath as it moves through your throat before you begin. Allowing the breath to go all the way through you a few times allows you to slow down and approach from a quiet inner landscape. Speak and listen to one another until you have arrived at a sweet spot where you both feel seen and heard.

---

84 "The Seven Principles for Making Marriage Work Quotes," Goodreads, accessed February 17, 2020.

Setting a timer can be helpful. A timer sets a boundary so you don't have to; think of your timer as a neutral party mediating the space. Communicating clearly with your partner about what you are feeling impacts their ability to respond effectively. Your partner can only understand when you share. After all, they are not a mind reader, even if they are highly attuned. I suggest you return to the vulnerability chapter, which offers insights into the value of being willing to risk sharing your true feelings. Use the tips there to practice taking risks while trusting that your partner will receive you with love.

Accept your partner and trust they are who they are and they may or may not step into their full potential. You can support them to grow by loving them and acknowledging they are on their own journey. Refrain from trying to control them. Stay in your heart and accept you both will have good times and bad times and we are all wildly eccentric—just in different ways. In a successful relationship, both partners will surrender to this as they accept each other and love one another just the way they are.

REMEMBER:

- Offer unconditional love and acceptance to your partner. It will make them feel safe.

- Accepting your partner and giving them space may mean dancing between being an ally who makes suggestions or being an observer who lets them find their way.

- Choose to be with your partner the way they already are, rather than as you would like them to be.

- Invest energy in learning about your partner; bring openness and curiosity as you relate.

- Use emotionally intelligent communication to create connection and avoid ruptures.

- Accept your partner's need for space, and don't take it personally.

- Be patient with yourself and your partner.

- Realize your partner won't meet all of your needs.

- Set an easy ask for your partner if your needs for contact differ.

- Communicate your needs regularly and from the heart.

UNCONDITIONAL ACCEPTANCE:
REFLECTION AND INTEGRATION WORKSHEET
(IT'S YOUR BOOK, FEEL FREE TO WRITE IN IT.)

I invite you to take a few minutes to write down two things that resonated for you in this chapter. Now, choose one to practice weekly. For the best results, look often at what you've written; your subconscious mind learns through repetition.

_____

_____

_____

_____

_____

_____

_____

_____

_____

_____

_____

CHAPTER 12

EVOLVING TOGETHER

———

"When two people relate to each other authentically and humanly, God is the electricity that surges between them."

- MARTIN BUBER

RELATIONSHIP AS AN EVOLUTIONARY PATH

Evolution is defined as, "the gradual development of something, especially from a simple to a more complex form."[85] Let's explore how you and your partner can become evolutionary allies on the journey of awakening to your true nature.

Gary and Tom have been allies on an evolutionary journey for more than twenty years. They have both been in extensive psychoanalysis and have done significant personal work in venues ranging from numerous self-inquiry seminars and Buddhist retreats to soul-stretching shamanic journeys. Doing this work deepened their ability to be present with themselves and each other, and to recognize

---

85 *Lexico*, s.v. "Evolution (n.)," accessed February 21, 2020.

everything that arises is a manifestation of their love. Tom quietly reflected:

> "When everything becomes an opportunity to recognize, to own, to act from, and to delight in our relationship, then the daily annoyances that arise get put into a larger perspective, and life becomes far more enjoyable. The pleasure of our love and our life together is multiplied. When socks on the floor can spark an experience of warm feeling or even of love, well, what a wonderful way to keep enjoying each other and what we have."

As you embark on a shared path of awakening, along the way you'll encounter each other's *shadow material* and neuroses; it is all a chance to grow. *Shadow material* is that which seems too painful to bear. Things you would rather leave in a locked box, tucked away behind clothes you haven't worn in years. In an evolutionary relationship, you agree to lovingly witness one another's shadows.

The process of unpacking your shadow has its own timing, and you cannot unsee what you've seen after looking deep inside. Be gentle with the process, and trust that if it's warranted, you may end up in pieces—the old container must be broken for something new to emerge.

We came here to evolve, to know love more deeply, and ultimately to realize our essential nature. "As far as we can discern, the sole purpose of human existence is to kindle a light of meaning in the darkness of mere being," wrote Swiss psychiatrist and psychoanalyst Carl Gustav Jung.[86]

Kathy and Lori's relationship is a spiritual practice. "Keep the questions bigger than the incidents," Kathy said. Their method of inquiry practice is a way to bring light to what is true.

Kathy contemplatively mused:

> "We see our relationship as a spiritual practice and that everything that happens, love it, hate it, like it, dislike it: everything is fodder. It's not being done to me, it is being done for me. We often ask each other, 'What if this was being done for you, not to you?' What is the growing edge if you really turn the question around for yourself?"

EVOLUTION IS A CHOICE

Being human is a privilege, and we do justice to this privilege by choosing to evolve. Your evolutionary journey points you to your own true nature, or what in the Buddhist tradition is called "Buddha Nature." When the Buddha reached enlightenment (or the full realization of his true nature), he realized all beings have the same nature, and that they have the capacity to wake up fully.

"Every sentient being—even insects—have Buddha nature," says His Holiness the Dalai Lama. "The seed of Buddha means consciousness, the cognitive power—the seed of

---

86   "C.G. Jung Quotes," Goodreads, accessed February 18, 2020.

enlightenment. That's from Buddha's viewpoint. All these destructive things can be removed from the mind, so therefore there's no reason to believe some sentient being cannot become Buddha. So every sentient being has that seed."[87]

Being in a relationship assists you in awakening because you have a partner with whom you can practice being conscious; you're doing reps in your *"relating dojo."* You will have opportunities to unveil the ways in which you are identified with your ego, take things personally, and are being held hostage by your conditioning. You are in it together and are allies on the path to true freedom.

John Welwood was an American clinical psychologist and psychotherapist known for having integrated psychological and spiritual concepts.[88] He spoke about the path of spiritual evolution, saying:

"We have to be willing to come apart at the seams, to be dismantled, to let our old ego structures fall apart before we can begin to embody sparks of the essential perfection at the core of our nature. To evolve spiritually, we have to allow these unworked, hidden, messy parts of ourselves to come to the surface."[89]

Dive deep within and discover who you really are underneath the tangled strands of hurt comprising your ego. In an evolutionary partnership, you commit to being present for the unwinding pain in both you and your partner. This process begins with knowing what you really want.

87 Dalai Lama [Tenzin Gyatso], "On Buddha Nature," *The Buddha* (blog), March 9, 2010.

88 "Biography," on John Welwood's official website, accessed May 24, 2020.

89 John Welwood, "Intimate Relationship as a Spiritual Crucible," on John Welwood's official website, accessed February 18, 2020.

Gary spoke beautifully about how this works in his relationship with Tom:

> *"The commitment started when I knew who I was, Tom knew who he was, then we knew who we were together. The critical thing was that from then on, we only wanted to make the other person feel whole, happy, and without pain in their lives. The commitment was to heal the other person as well as ourselves."*

THE HOLY FIRE OF TRUE INTIMACY

An intimate relationship has the potential to open you to universal Love, which knows no bounds and is a gateway to the divine.

When both partners choose to be present and vulnerable with one another, the doorway to a kind of luminous intimacy may open.

If it does, you may be graced with an experience of timelessness in which all separation disappears. Your relationship has become a spiritual practice and together, you are tilling the earth in the garden of presence.

Tom and Gary have a truly intimate partnership. Tilling the garden of their relationship took the form of deep dives as well as individual personal work. "If you've got a place to work through your own shit, and to own it, you don't have to act it out with your partner," Gary said, "and we did our best to own our own shit."

The last thing they wanted to do was wound each other, so they learned early on to communicate with clarity. It was a process. "We did a lot of deep work together," Tom said, "sitting knee to knee and face-to-face speaking our truth to each other with blazing, painful, and even shocking honesty."

To move your relationship to a new level, you have to shift old ways of being—but it only takes one of you to initiate change. There is a dance between your inner evolution and your shared evolution. As one partner evolves, the partnership dynamic evolves as well. "To gain greater access to the gold of our nature in relationship," John Welwood writes, "a certain alchemy is required: the refining of our conditioned defensive patterns. The good news is that this alchemy generated between two people also furthers a larger alchemy within them."[90]

Here is how this worked in the case of a client of mine, Michael. Michael was born and raised in New England, in a home where it was unacceptable for men to show vulnerability. He learned from his father that anger was the only masculine emotion. He never saw his father cry or show fear. When he was in a relationship, he believed he needed to be "strong" in order to be loved and believed he could not show his more tender emotions to his partner. He believed that if he appeared weak or vulnerable, he would be seen as less than a real man and be abandoned.

---

90 Ibid.

Michael shifted away from his family of origin template by working on himself through therapy and meditative practices. And over time, he learned all of his emotions needed acknowledgement and a space to be held. Not just anger. As he witnessed other men he respected being able to show vulnerability, his outdated ideas about what a "real" man was evolved into a much more complete model of masculinity. He now saw he could allow himself to be both strong and vulnerable, and he said:

> "A huge shift happened when I learned that I could set aside the judgements about being vulnerable that would arise when I was wanting to be held by my partner when I was feeling sadness or fear. I could just set them aside and let myself cry like a baby. What a blessing to be held in this way!"

Previously, Michael wanted to have sex much more often than his partner Josie did, which can often be the case due to different testosterone levels.

When Michael began to be vulnerable with Josie, he no longer felt dissatisfied. With a feeling of peaceful relief he could say, "What I am mainly wanting from the sexual connection is intimacy. It's amazing to feel so exposed, connected, and intimate—and recognize that it's not dependent on having sex."

Michael discovered it was safe to be seen in his vulnerability and found freedom in the awareness that his partner would not leave him. A new level of intimacy beyond anything they had previously experienced opened up for both of them.

Along the relationship journey, it's possible to discover places of pure ecstasy born out of the communion of heart and body, places you would not stumble into if you had not said, "I'm all in, I am all in for Love."

Sexuality can play an important role in this evolution, and these pleasure-filled realms can be scary if unfamiliar.

An intimate sexual exploration based in presence and passion can open you in ways you could not possibly have imagined.

In my experience this depth of physical, emotional, and spiritual union can deliver you into an elevated state of consciousness.

Our local shaman, Tomás, offered his wisdom regarding how to enter into the sacred realms of higher lovemaking:

> *"If you stay in the relationship, do the work, keep your heart open, and continue growing, you can reach the realms of higher lovemaking. So, for all the joys of lovemaking and the physical plane sensations, there is a deeper level of lovemaking which transcends this, but you won't get there unless you stay the course."*

The more committed you are to one another, the more deeply you will be able to open to the deliciously pleasure-filled depths of heart-based intimacy. In the union of spirituality and lovemaking, it's possible for the *"other"* to disappear. This may lead you to untold sexual, sensual, and soulful delights that deliver you to higher planes of consciousness.

Stephen and Ondrea Levine spoke to this in their groundbreaking book, *Embracing the Beloved*. "Before we know who we are, we make love to another," they wrote. "When we know who we are, we are that other—love itself."[91] The Levines described their conscious love-making as a sort of "ecstatic oneness." When you know who you truly are, sexuality shifts from being about fulfilling physical needs and becomes about communion with love and a soulful longing for the Beloved—and ultimately for a union with the Divine itself.

LOVE IS AN INSIDE JOB

When my partner offers me steady, loving presence, my defensiveness decreases and any reactivity softens. What I have realized is that most of the things that challenge me in my relationship are from my own past hurts, and the ways I've learned to cope with them. Love is an inside job, and my efforts to become aware of my subconscious patterns alleviate the need to repeat old, obscenely boring and exhausting dramas.

As shadow material moves from your subconscious to your conscious mind, you become more self-aware and more self-responsible. You'll discover that with awareness comes responsibility because you can no longer wiggle out of places

---

91   Stephen Levine and Ondrea Levine, *Embracing the Beloved: Relationship as a Path of Awakening* (New York: Anchor Books, 1996), 162.

once you see them for what they are. That's why people often say, *"Ignorance is bliss."* It's not really bliss; it's a place where you are unaware, which offers an easy out. When you become aware, however, then you are responsible.

You take responsibility for your actions and remain aware of what is happening internally. For example, when your partner is upset, rather than withdrawing by leaving the room or blocking them, you can connect to how much you care about them and offer spacious, loving presence while they calm down. In being compassionate and self-responsible, you create your own happiness. You aren't separate from spacious presence; the vastness of conscious awareness makes room for each of you to own your own stuff, much in the way that the desert sky makes room for storms to pass then returns to its eternal blueness—clear and undisturbed.

Lori makes room for Kathy's feelings in this way:

> *"It's not that we don't get on each other's nerves. Our fears come up and we may act badly with each other at times, but there's a kind of letting it wash over me, rather than pushing back. Having boundaries and knowing that if Kathy's acting out, she's in pain. I don't take it personally because I know she's suffering about something, and that's how it's expressing itself."*

My ex Clark's story also points to how he learned to love himself and become self-responsible. When he was in his early twenties, his first wife had an affair with his best friend. When Clark discovered this, he blurted out, "Okay, I'm walking out the door." He wasn't open to doing any repair; he took the affair personally, as if the fact that they'd gotten together had been a ploy to get rid of him. Once the sting wore off, Clark could see that their connection had nothing to do with him.

Years later, he experienced another betrayal with his second wife when, after they divorced, she moved in with a close friend. This time, however, Clark had become wiser and less ego-identified after going to therapy, joining a men's group, and practicing mindful self-inquiry. He did not succumb to his old story of being rejected or interpret her betrayal to mean that he was "fatally flawed."

Clark is a huge movie buff and he told me about a dramatic movie scene where the woman has an affair, her husband finds out about it, and flies into a rage. She is hysterically crying and calling to him, "Come back, come back." As Clark is watching the movie, he sees the husband storm out in anger, and thinks to himself, "Dude. You should really just hear her out and not feel so damn bad about this. This is the heaviest blow you can imagine and it's totally not about you." Clark had earned an evolutionarily upgraded, drama-free response. In life, it is wise to play the cards we are dealt, as though they are the ones we had always wanted.

"To bow to the fact of our life's sorrows and betrayals is to accept them; and from this deep gesture we discover that all life is workable," writes Jack Kornfield, a renowned meditation teacher and founder of Spirit Rock Meditation Center. "As we learn to bow, we discover that the heart holds more freedom and compassion than we could imagine."[92]

---

92 "Jack Kornfield Quotes," Goodreads, accessed February 11, 2020.

Being in a healthy relationship means being willing to do your inner work. It was our old friend Danny who said, "This whole thing is about how willing you are to increase your self-awareness. That is the total issue." The more loving and compassionate you can be with yourself, the more you can be this way with your partner.

It takes a commitment to yourself to grow the muscles of love and compassion. In much the same way that you would strengthen a certain muscle group at the gym, you also strengthen the inner muscles of love and compassion. You have to do the reps. Find a partner who can be patient with you while you do your reps and who is willing to do their own; it takes dedication and practice to grow these muscles.

My own life and relationship provide me with plenty of opportunities to strengthen these muscles, starting with being loving and compassionate with myself. In moments where it feels like my partner is distant and I want to feel more connected to him, I recognize he's just being himself, and I wrap my own warm, compassionate arms around the young part of myself who wants to feel loved. I also have compassion for my partner because I am aware his way of loving is linked to what he experienced when he was younger, too.

"In any moment we can learn to let go of hatred and fear," says Jack Kornfield. "We can rest in peace, love, and forgiveness. It is never too late. Yes, to sustain love we need to develop practices that strengthen the natural compassion within us."[93]

---

93 Ibid.

MINDFUL AWARENESS

Mindful awareness supports evolution and growth, which both happen within the appearance of linear time. Being in a partnership with someone who is committed to their awakening, to stabilizing in presence, and to being in timelessness together means you understand the infinite is the space in which the play of consciousness unfolds. In the Hindu tradition, consciousness incarnates into form in order to play. This is what is known as the *Divine Leela*, which is Sanskrit for "the divine play of god." In this play you have an opportunity to align your heart with pure awareness and to know yourself as this, that which does not need to evolve. What comes and goes is as sacred as what doesn't come and go.

Enjoy the play of being in a relationship. Respond to the invitation to awaken together and live life fully.

Relationships hold an incredible evolutionary potential because they insist you be present and respond, rather than impulsively react. They ask you to be curious and to discover *what is* beyond making assumptions. In an evolutionary relationship, there is enough safety to allow for vulnerability—both around the tender hurts and the magnificent truth of who you are.

When you relate to one another as consciousness or pure awareness, there is room for your pain because consciousness is infinitely bigger than your pain. This is what spiritual teacher Eckhart Tolle calls "the pain body." When you have the awareness that you are consciousness relating to consciousness itself, your relationship becomes the ground for a kind of healing that cannot be done on a meditation cushion. Your committed relationship then becomes the final frontier, a place where you can challenge old patterns and relax into fulfilled joy.

Through meditative practice, being willing to peel away emotional baggage and work with your shadow material, both parties will eventually shift their center of gravity away from the ego-identified self—who has been hurt, is ashamed, and does not recognize their own essential lovability—to the one who has realized their essential nature. And your essential nature is *already* free; this does not mean you won't experience pain or hurt, but it means you will suffer for less time when it does appear.

Let us review some of what we discussed in this chapter. A committed relationship has the potential to be an evolutionary journey, one in which you might grow into the best version of yourself. Along the way, you will have a chance to look at your shadow material, and to welcome it into the light.

When you are in an evolutionary relationship, it is possible to share profoundly transformative sexual and spiritual experiences. In the experience of complete union, the "other" dissolves. A relationship opens you to a type of healing you will not find by sitting on a meditation cushion. The growth process may be blissful, painful or both. No matter what, remember you and your partner are allies on the journey of awakening.

REMEMBER:

- Commit to your partnership and it will serve your healing and evolution.

- Be aware and practice compassion, kindness, and self-responsibility.

- Meditate regularly to shift your center of gravity away from your ego-identified self to your true self.

- Be mindful: it is a key to your evolution.

- The more fully you commit to one another, the more you open to extraordinary depths of intimacy.

- Do the reps needed to strengthen your love and compassion muscles.

- Refrain from taking things personally; it's not about you.

- Be willing to look at your shadow materials as your partner holds a space of loving presence.

- Stay the course; show up fully and the doorway to the higher realms of lovemaking will open.

- Celebrate the fact that you have found someone to evolve with.

EVOLVING TOGETHER:
REFLECTION AND INTEGRATION WORKSHEET
(IT'S YOUR BOOK, FEEL FREE TO WRITE IN IT.)

I invite you to take a few minutes to write down two things that resonated for you in this chapter. Now, choose one to practice weekly. For the best results, look often at what you've written; your subconscious mind learns through repetition.

_____

_____

_____

_____

_____

_____

_____

_____

_____

_____

CONCLUSION

———

Writing this book has changed me; it's softened my sharp edges and opened my heart wider to love. I have become more skilled at relating to the gentle, extremely patient man who has mysteriously appeared to walk with me as my partner in life. I'm the first to admit that hanging out with little ol' New-York-powerhouse me is no small thing. Until now, I hadn't met anyone up to the task. I am more dedicated to staying the course than I have ever been. My willingness to take responsibility and clean up my own mess has most assuredly contributed to the success of our relationship.

The lusciously rich and infinitely nuanced path of loving is often fraught with growth opportunities. These invite us to shift from looking through an egotistical lens to seeing with the eyes of the true heart, which is trustworthy. The mind is a trickster who can wreak havoc on a relationship when you fall under its spell, believing you are your pain—which you are not. You can heal in the safe space of a loving relationship.

Having read this book, you now know I've been snagged by my own pain and arrogance plenty, and that being in a committed relationship has humbled and grown me profoundly. It has invited me to turn over every stone and look closely at myself, to be honest and in integrity while maintaining clear boundaries. Evolving into the best version of oneself is itself the ultimate reward.

So, have hope, revisit the worksheets in this book—hang them on your wall and look at them. Deepen your understanding. Apply the practical wisdom you've received in the good times and especially when you feel challenged. And if you are at your limit and want to give up, pause, breathe deeply, and move slowly; change happens one step at a time.

My hope is that you practice the things you've learned. That they support you to expand your ability to be loving with yourself and others, that untold sweetness becomes woven into the fabric of your daily experience with your partner, and ultimately that your relationship becomes permanently altered in ways that are fulfilling, evolve you, and continue to enrich your life.

Lean into uncertainty, keep your heart open—catch yourself when you fall into an old trance or feel the urge to reenact old dramas. Accept yourself and your partner, and most of all, love yourself, love large, and embrace the vastness of who you are. Your place on the path of luminous intimacy awaits, no one else can fill it.

READER'S RESOURCES, IN ADDITION TO THE BOOKS IN THE APPENDIX.

ABUSIVE RELATIONSHIPS AND ADDICTIONS

AA Services. *Alcoholics Anonymous Big Book*. New York: Alcoholics Anonymous World Services, 2002.

Brown, Nina W. *Children of the Self-Absorbed: A Grown-Up's Guide to Getting over Narcissistic Parents*. Oakland: New Harbinger Publications, 2008.

Davis, Laura. *Allies in Healing : When the Person You Love Is a Survivor of Child Sexual Abuse*. New York: HarperCollins Publishers, 1991.

Forward, Susan. *Toxic Parents : Overcoming Their Hurtful Legacy & Reclaiming Your Life*. Bantam: Bantam Doubleday Dell Publishing Group, 2002.

Stosny, Steven. *Love without Hurt: Turn Your Resentful, Angry, or Emotionally Abusive Relationship into a Compassionate, Loving One.* Philadelphia: Ingram Publisher Services, 2008.

Whitfield, Charles L. *Healing the Child Within: Discovery and Recovery for Adult Children of Dysfunctional Families.* Deerfield Beach: Health Communications, 1989.

ATTACHMENT THEORY
Bowlby, John. *Separation: Anxiety And Anger.* New York: Ingram Publisher Services, 1976.

Heller, Rachel, and Amir Levine. *Attached: The New Science of Adult Attachment and How It Can Help You Find—and Keep—Love.* Los Angeles: Penguin Putnam, 2018.

Johnson, Sue. *Hold Me Tight: Your Guide to the Most Successful Approach to Building Loving Relationships.* London: Little, Brown Book Group, 2011.

Johnson, Sue. *Love Sense: The Revolutionary New Science of Romantic Relationships.* New York: Little, Brown Spark, 2013.

CO-DEPENDENCY
Beattie, Melody. *Codependent No More.* Center City: Hazelden Information & Educational Services, 2006.

FEMINIST PSYCHOLOGY
Benjamin, Jessica. *The Bonds of Love: Psychoanalysis, Feminism and the Problems of Domination.* New York: Random House USA, 1988.

POLYAMORY
Hardy, Janet W., and Dossie Easton. *The Ethical Slut: A Practical Guide to Polyamory, Open Relationships, and Other in Sex and Love.* Berkeley: Ten Speed Press, 2019.

RELATIONSHIPS
Hendrix, Harville, and Helen Hunt. *Getting the Love You Want: A Guide for Couples.* New York: Saint Martin's Press, 2019.

Neff, Kristin. *Self Compassion.* London: Hodder & Stoughton, 2011.

TRAUMA
Herman, Judith. *Trauma and Recovery: The Aftermath of Violence—from Domestic Abuse to Political Terror.* New York: Ingram Publisher Services, 2015.

Levine, Peter A. *In an Unspoken Voice.* Berkeley: North Atlantic Books, 2015.

Levine, Peter A. *Waking the Tiger.* Berkeley: North Atlantic Books, 2017.

Van der Kolk, Bessel. *The Body Keeps the Score: Mind, Brain and Body in the Transformation of Trauma*. London: Penguin Books, 2015.

APPENDIX

EPIGRAPH
Sagan, Carl. *Contact*. New York: Simon and Schuster, 1985.

INTRODUCTION
McKinley Irvin Family Law. "32 Shocking Divorce Statistics." *Family Law Blog*. Updated 2018. https://www.mckinleyirvin.com/family-law-blog/2012/october/32-shocking-divorce-statistics/.

CHAPTER 1
Castro, Giovanna. "The Neuroscience of Love." *Emotion, Brain, & Behavior Laboratory*. December 8, 2014. https://sites.tufts.edu/emotiononthebrain/2014/12/08/the-neuroscience-of-love/.

Devaney, Jacob. "The Neurobiology of Love and Relationships." *UPLIFT*. January 14, 2016. https://upliftconnect.com/neurobiology-of-love/.

Esch, Tobias, and George B. Stefano. "The Neurobiology of Love." *Neuroendocrinology Letters* 26, No. 3 (June 2005): 175-192. http://www.nel.edu/the-neurobiology-of-love-1981/.

Goodreads. "Wired for Love Quotes." Accessed February 6, 2020. https://www.goodreads.com/work/quotes/18416750-wired-for-love.

Liu, C.J. "How to build intimacy? (Stan Tatkin)." *Fire it up with CJ*. Published June 22, 2015. https://www.fireitupwithcj.com/how-to-build-intimacy-in-marriage-and-relationships-stan-tatkin/.

Psychologist World. "Attachment Theory." Developmental Psychology. Accessed February 5, 2020. https://www.psychologistworld.com/developmental/attachment-theory.

Tatkin, Stan. *Your Brain on Love: The Neurobiology of Healthy Relationships.* Read by author. Louisville: Sounds True Publishing, 2013. Audio CD, 5 hr., 50 min.

Tatkin, Stan, and Tracey Boldemann-Tatkin. "What Does It Mean to Be in a Secure-Functioning Relationship? And Why Should It Matter to Me?" *Shambhala Mountain Center* (blog), August 14, 2019. https://blog.shambhalamountain.org/what-does-it-mean-to-be-in-a-secure-functioning-relationship-and-why-should-it-matter-to-me/.

Wu, Katherine. "Love, Actually: The science behind lust, attraction, and companionship." *Science in the News.* Harvard University. February 14, 2017. http://sitn.hms.harvard.edu/flash/2017/love-actually-science-behind-lust-attraction-companionship/.

CHAPTER 2

Brittle, Zach. "The Positive Perspective." *The Gottman Institute* (blog). April 8, 2015. https://www.gottman.com/blog/the-positive-perspective/.

Goodreads. "Eight Dates Quotes." Accessed January 18, 2020. https://www.goodreads.com/work/quotes/59198136-eight-dates.

Goodreads. "Men Are from Mars, Women Are from Venus Quotes." Accessed January 18, 2020. https://www.goodreads.com/work/quotes/55001-men-are-from-mars-women-are-from-venus-a-practical-guide-for-improvin.

Goodreads. "We Do Quotes." Accessed January 18, 2020. https://www.goodreads.com/work/quotes/55357157-we-do-saying-yes-to-a-relationship-of-depth-true-connection-and-endur.

Goodreads. "Wired for Love Quotes." Accessed February 6, 2020. https://www.goodreads.com/work/quotes/18416750-wired-for-love.

Robbins, Tony's official website. "The 20 best quotes about relationships by Tony Robbins." Accessed January 14, 2020. https://www.tonyrobbins.com/tony-robbins-quotes/relationship-quotes/.

Tatkin, Stan. *Your Brain on Love: The Neurobiology of Healthy Relationships.* Read by author. Louisville: Sounds True Publishing, 2013. Audio CD, 5 hr., 50 min.

CHAPTER 3

Dictionary.com. s.v. "Crucible." Accessed January 27, 2020. https://www.dictionary.com/browse/crucible?s=t.

George, Mary Beth. "What Does Trust and Commitment Look Like in a Relationship?" *The Gottman Institute* (blog). March 6, 2019. https://www.gottman.com/blog/what-does-trust-and-commitment-look-like-in-a-relationship/.

Jamison, Abby. "20 Love Quotes to Remind You to Stay Together—Even When Times Get Really, Really Tough." *Your Tango.* January 8, 2018. https://www.yourtango.com/2017304667/best-love-quotes-relationship-tough-times.

Johnson, Sue. "Ten Tips for a Strong Vibrant Relationship." Ottawa Couple & Family Institute. October 2, 2017.
https://www.ocfi.ca/ten-tips-for-a-strong-vibrant-relationship/.

Vocabulary.com. "Commitment." Dictionary. Accessed April 29, 2020.
https://www.vocabulary.com/dictionary/commitment.

CHAPTER 4

Goodreads. "We Do Quotes." Accessed January 18, 2020.
https://www.goodreads.com/work/quotes/55357157-we-do-saying-yes-to-a-relationship-of-depth-true-connection-and-endur.

London Real. "DR. JOE DISPENZA - BREAK THE HABIT OF BEING YOU - Part 1/2." May 8, 2019. Video, 46:10.
https://www.youtube.com/watch?v=RYfjz-etukA.

Schoultz, Mike. "John Wooden Leadership Qualities: 14 He Used for Career Development." *Digital Spark Marketing* (blog). January 8, 2016.
https://digitalsparkmarketing.com/john-wooden-leadership-qualities/.

Yalim, Deniz. "88+ Best Teamwork Quotes to Celebrate Collaboration." *BayArt* (blog). September 21, 2019.
https://bayart.org/top-teamwork-quotes-celebrate-collaboration/.

CHAPTER 5

AZ Quotes. "Rachel Naomi Remen Inspirational Quotes." Accessed January 21, 2020.
https://www.azquotes.com/author/17862-Rachel_Naomi_Remen/tag/inspirational.

Gottman, John M. *The Science of Trust: Emotional Attunement for Couples.* New York: W. W. Norton & Company, 2011.

Goodreads. "Men Are from Mars, Women Are from Venus Quotes." Accessed January 18, 2020.
https://www.goodreads.com/work/quotes/55001-men-are-from-mars-women-are-from-venus-a-practical-guide-for-improvin.

Goodreads. "The Science of Trust Quotes." Accessed May 22, 2020.
https://www.goodreads.com/work/quotes/15559902-the-science-of-trust-emotional-attunement-for-couples.

Gruber, Elon. "Synopsis of the Ted Talks on 4 Habits of All Successful Relationships." The Counseling & Wellness Center of Wyomissing. October 28, 2919.
https://thecounselingandwellnesscenterofwyo.com/synopsis-of-the-ted-talks-on-4-habits-of-all-successful-relationships/.

Nassar, Carl. "The Importance of Feeling Understood." *Heart-Centered Counseling* (blog). December 22,2016.
https://carlscounseling.com/the-importance-of-feeling-understood/.

Taylor-Cummings, Andrea. "The 4 Habits of ALL Successful Relationships." The 4 Habits (blog). Accessed January 21, 2020.
https://the4habits.com/the-4-habits-of-all-successful-relationships/.

CHAPTER 6

5 Love Languages. "Discover Your Love Language." Accessed on June 20, 2020.
https://www.5lovelanguages.com/.

Adamski, Carol. "Living in Gratitude: Appreciation Is Glue for Relationships."
Gratitude Habitat (blog). October 15, 2016.
https://gratitudehabitat.com/2016/10/living-in-gratitude-appreciation-is-glue-for-relationships/.

Blondin, Sarah. "Access Your Inner Source of Hope," January 1, 2020. Insight Timer, 3:03.
https://soundcloud.com/liveawakepodcast/s02-make-it-sacred.

Feloni, Richard. "Tim Ferriss Lives His Life According to an Ancient Greek Quote
That Helps Him Prepare for the Worst." *Business Insider*. December 1, 2017.
https://www.businessinsider.com/tim-ferriss-favorite-quote-greek-philosopher-archilochus-2017-12.

Johnson, Sue. "Ten Tips for a Strong Vibrant Relationship." Ottawa Couple & Family
Institute. October 2, 2017.
https://www.ocfi.ca/ten-tips-for-a-strong-vibrant-relationship/.

Pitt, Julia. "The Deepest Principle of Human Nature Is a Craving to Be Appreciated."
The Royal Gazette. May 7, 2013.
http://www.royalgazette.com/article/20130507/COLUMN21/705079979.

CHAPTER 7

BrainyQuote. "Bryant H. McGill Quotes." Accessed February 3, 2020.
https://www.brainyquote.com/quotes/bryant_h_mcgill_168276.

Conscious Life. "Dr. Joe Dispenza – 'Your personality creates your personal reality.'"
March 27, 2017. Video, 3:01.
https://www.youtube.com/watch?v=qrozom9CI4Q.

Dispenza, Dr. Joe. "Week-Long Advanced Retreat." Lecture, Santa Fe, New Mexico,
February, 2018.

Lisitsa, Ellie. "The Love Lab." *The Gottman Institute* (blog). August 1, 2012.
https://www.gottman.com/blog/what-makes-love-last-the-love-lab/.

Miller, Kori D. "14 Health Benefits of Practicing Gratitude According to Science."
Positive Psychology (blog). April 16, 2020.
https://positivepsychology.com/benefits-of-gratitude/.

Poole Heller, Diane. "Strengthen Relationships with Repair." *Dr. Diane Poole Heller*
(blog). Accessed May 29, 2020.
https://dianepooleheller.com/strengthen-relationships-with-repair/.

Stracqualursi, Veronica. "RBG Was Married for More Than 50 Years. J.Lo Asked Her
for Marriage Advice." *CNN*. August 31, 2019.
https://edition.cnn.com/2019/08/31/politics/jennifer-lopez-ruth-bader-ginsburg-marriage-advice.

Whyte, David. *Consolations: The Solace, Nourishment and Underlying Meaning of
Everyday Words*. Langley: Many Rivers Press, 2014.

CHAPTER 8

Chou, Jessica. "Is Honesty ALWAYS The Best Policy?" Refinery 29. July 8, 2015. https://www.refinery29.com/en-us/honesty-in-relationships.

Goodreads. "Thin Book of Trust Quotes." Accessed April 18, 2020. https://www.goodreads.com/work/quotes/7259412-thin-book-of-trust.

Hatvani, Ondina N. "A.R.E. You There? What Is the Secret Ingredient That Makes a Relationship Thrive?" *Ondina Wellness* (blog). Accessed May 28, 2020. https://ondinawellness.com/are-you-there/.

Johnson, Sue's official website. "What Is a Secure Bond?" Accessed February 10, 2020. https://www.drsuejohnson.com/love/what-is-a-secure-bond/ (page discontinued).

Key, Joel. "BRAVING: Brené Brown's Acronym for Building Trust," *Bloomsoup* (blog), accessed May 25, 2020. https://bloomsoup.com/braving-brene-brown/.

Taylor, Jane. "Vulnerability Is…." *Habits for Wellbeing* (blog). Accessed February 8, 2020. https://www.habitsforwellbeing.com/vulnerability-is/.

Whitman, Walt. *Leaves of Grass*. London: Penguin Books Ltd, 2017.

CHAPTER 9

Benson, Kyle. "The Magic Relationship Ratio, According to Science." *The Gottman Institute* (blog). October 4, 2017. https://www.gottman.com/blog/the-magic-relationship-ratio-according-science/.

BrainyQuote. "Viktor E. Frankl Quotes." Accessed December 11, 2019. https://www.brainyquote.com/authors/viktor-e-frankl-quotes.

Family Action Network. "John and Julie Gottman: *Eight Dates: Essential Conversations for a Lifetime of Love*." Interview by Eli Finkel. March 13, 2019, video, 44:07, March 16, 2019. https://www.youtube.com/watch?v=V8XlHGHP98I.

Fronsdal, Gil. *The Issue at Hand: Essays on Buddhist Mindfulness Practice*. Redwood City: Insight Meditation Center, 2008.

Goodreads. "Alone Together Quotes." Accessed June 4, 2020. https://www.goodreads.com/work/quotes/13566692-alone-together-why-we-expect-more-from-technology-and-less-from-each-ot.

Goodreads. "Love Is Letting Go of Fear Quotes." Accessed February 11, 2020. https://www.goodreads.com/work/quotes/181354-love-is-letting-go-of-fear.

Goodreads. "Sherry Turkle Quotes." Accessed May 26, 2020. https://www.goodreads.com/author/quotes/153503.Sherry_Turkle.

Hendricks Institute. "Openness to Hearing the Truth." Accessed on January 21, 2020. https://hendricks.com/links/L314_Openness-Hearing-Truth.pdf

Johnson, Sue. "Ten Tips for a Strong Vibrant Relationship." Ottawa Couple & Family Institute. October 2, 2017. https://www.ocfi.ca/ten-tips-for-a-strong-vibrant-relationship/.

Respiratory Therapy Zone. "99 Awesome Quotes About Breathing (Respiratory Therapist Edition)." Accessed May 26, 2020. https://www.respiratorytherapyzone.com/quotes-about-breathing/.

TEDx Talks. "Relationships are Hard, But Why? | Stan Tatkin | TEDxKC." September 2, 2016.Video, 10:13. https://www.youtube.com/watch?v=2xKXLPuju8U&feature=youtu.be.

CHAPTER 10

Neace, Cassandra. "25 Dr. Seuss Quotes to Remind You to Be Good and Do Good." *Book Riot.* July 30, 2018. https://bookriot.com/2018/07/30/dr-seuss-quotes/.

Newport Academy. "Why Laughter Is Good for Mental Health." March 30, 2018. https://www.newportacademy.com/resources/mental-health/laughter-good-for-you/.

PsychAlive. "Laugh it Up: Why Laughing Brings Us Closer Together." Accessed February 14, 2020. https://www.psychalive.org/laugh-it-up-why-laughing-brings-us-closer-together/.

Schoenwald, Christine. "How Laughter Improves Your Relationship, Because LOLing Is like Taking a Mini Spa Day for Your Emotions." *Bustle.* April 10, 2015. https://www.bustle.com/articles/75352-how-laughter-improves-your-relationship-because-loling-is-like-taking-a-mini-spa-day-for-your.

Whyte, David. *Consolations: The Solace, Nourishment and Underlying Meaning of Everyday Words.* Langley: Many Rivers Press, 2014.

CHAPTER 11

Goodreads. "Eight Dates Quotes." Accessed January 18, 2020. https://www.goodreads.com/work/quotes/59198136-eight-dates.

Goodreads. "The Seven Principles for Making Marriage Work Quotes." Accessed February 17, 2020. https://www.goodreads.com/work/quotes/4370-the-seven-principles-for-making-marriage-work-a-practical-guide-from-th.

Merriam-Webster. s.v. "Grok (v.)." Accessed February 16, 2020. https://www.merriam-webster.com/dictionary/grok.

Richo, David. *How to Be an Adult in Relationships.* Boston: Shambala Publications, 2002.

CHAPTER 12

Dalai Lama [Tenzin Gyatso]. "On Buddha Nature." *The Buddha* (blog). March 9, 2010. https://www.pbs.org/thebuddha/blog/2010/Mar/9/dalai-lama-buddha-nature/.

Goodreads. "C.G. Jung Quotes." Accessed February 18, 2020. https://www.goodreads.com/author/quotes/38285.C_G_Jung.

Goodreads. "Jack Kornfield Quotes." Accessed February 11, 2020. https://www.goodreads.com/author/quotes/59705.Jack_Kornfield.

Levine, Stephen, and Ondrea Levine. *Embracing the Beloved: Relationship as a Path of Awakening*. New York: Anchor Books, 1996.

Lexico. s.v. "Evolution (n.)." Accessed February 21, 2020. https://www.lexico.com/en/definition/evolution.

Welwood, John. "Intimate Relationship as a Spiritual Crucible." John Welwood's official website. Accessed February 18, 2020. http://www.johnwelwood.com/articles/Relationship_as_a_Spiritual_Crucible_website.pdf.

Welwood, John's official website. "Biography." Accessed May 24, 2020. http://www.johnwelwood.com/biography.htm.

Made in the USA
San Bernardino, CA
12 August 2020

76987998R00122